ANOTHER GENERATION ALMOST FORGOTTEN

ANOTHER GENERATION ALMOST FORGOTTEN

Jefferson Wiggins

To order additional copies of this book, contact:
Xlibris Corporation
1-888-795-4274
www.Xlibris.com
Orders@Xlibris.com
18630

This book is dedicated to my wife, Janice,
whose wise counsel made the publication of this book possible.
Her incessant prodding and belief in me was crucial in helping me
to recall a life that would have been easier for me to forget.

ACKNOWLEDGMENTS

The author gratefully acknowledges his appreciation to Laura Pettinato whose skills and dedication resulted in the writing of *Hearts of Believers,* the screenplay adaptation of this work.

FOREWORD

I vividly remember the night of September 17, 2000. It was the night I first met Dr. Jefferson Wiggins. Jeff and a few select members of the community had applied to fill a vacancy on the New Fairfield, Connecticut, Board of Education. The other board members and I were impressed with Jeff's credentials, his background, and his personality. Jeff was an extremely charismatic, well-educated man—a man who was a scholar, an educator, and a war veteran. We didn't need to think twice about filling our vacancy. Jeff was clearly the ideal candidate and he was unanimously approved for board membership that very evening.

For the next two months, I thought I got to know Jeff pretty well as we worked side by side on various board-related issues. Jeff's dedication to the board and his desire to fulfill his obligations as a board member were always impressive. Jeff also had a keen ongoing interest in volunteering at our schools, as a mentor to young second grade children. I always admired how he selflessly gave of himself, above and beyond his duties as a board member. I didn't know at the time that Jeff was fulfilling a vow he'd made over fifty years ago—a vow to his own personal mentors.

I first heard the story you're about to read on a snowy night in November. Jeff and I were driving to a school board training conference. The weather was foul and what should have been a two-hour trip turned into four hours of treacherous road travel. Jeff and I were talking about all sorts of things and he happened to mention he was writing a book. He asked me if I'd like to give it a read. When I inquired what it was about, he told me it was his personal story about his experiences in World War II and his friendship during that time with a Staten Island librarian and an ailing Catholic Priest. When Jeff mentioned that the Ku Klux Klan had come to hang his father when he was six years old and that he was only a young teen when he ran away from home and joined the Army, I was both stunned and intrigued. Here I was, sitting in a jeep with my peer, someone I thought was a seemingly ordinary person. I understood then that there was more to Jeff than I realized. Much lay beneath the surface of this mild-mannered, good-humored man. Obviously, he had led an extraordinary life.

I read Jeff's story in one sitting, and was moved to tears. His life experience is a valuable lesson for us all. His is a remarkable story of a boy without hope whose life was changed, if not saved, by a series of events and a few exceptional individuals who believed he had the ability to lead, the ability to make a difference in this world.

Jeff is living proof that any child can excel and become "somebody" through hard work and perseverance. As a child, Jeff's life was filled with poverty, hunger, and pain. He had no formal education beyond the sixth or seventh grade. Yet, despite lacking material things and the opportunities so many of us take for granted, Jeff always maintained the single most important thing of all—an intense desire to learn and the will to make something of himself. His story reminds us all that regardless of how dire our circumstances may seem, if we believe in ourselves, there will always be others who believe in us and support us in our life choices.

In life, many paths may appear before us. Each and every one of us has the power and responsibility to select the path that will lead us to personal success. Now I understood fully Jeff's intense desire to work with young children. This conscience-driven, moral, and inspired man was fulfilling his promises to his mentors.

Jeff's story explores the roots of hate and racism and serves as a reminder that, as individuals, we all have the ability to help our nation achieve social harmony. We must remember that hate and intolerance are learned behaviors, behaviors that our children must not learn. Our children are our most precious resource and they alone will carry our messages from generation to generation. With time comes progress, with progress comes change, with change comes understanding, and with understanding comes respect.

We have the power and responsibility as parents, as educators, as mentors, as human beings to make a formidable impact on future generations. Let us use our power wisely, to see that we don't cripple future generations with the veil of ignorance and social intolerance that has plagued our country for centuries.

Dr. Erich J. Stegmeier

AUTHOR'S NOTE

This story is substantially based on facts. I say "substantially" because it was not written from notes or records but rather from memories. At the time of the most compelling and formative experiences of this story, I was young, uneducated and unsophisticated. I had little vision of a future for myself, much less a vision that more than fifty years into the future I would have any reason to write these words or that others would have any reason to read them. So this work is built from memories. Over the years, some memories have faded, others have crystallized, and still others have been shaped by the perspective of time, experience and emotion.

The story is as I remember it, as I remember experiencing it. Some may remember it differently. Others may choose to forget altogether because of the pain and humiliation that is involved.

This story is written in the third person, yet it is about me. I have used the real names of characters. In writing this story, I found myself alternating between the first and third persons. Some memories were too painful to commit to paper in the first person. Yet the experiences upon which this work is based were far too personal to ascribe to characters with fictitious names. So the work stands as it is. This struggle for perspective, in itself, speaks volumes to the impact of these events and memories on my life.

ANOTHER GENERATION ALMOST FORGOTTEN

Jefferson Wiggins

"He wept that we might weep—
Each wrong demands a tear."

Lazarus,
at the tomb of Jesus

CHAPTER ONE

The tall, red-faced sergeant barely looked at the skinny black boy standing before him in his small office at the United States Post Office. After all, didn't they all look the same?

Jeff Wiggins was a young delivery boy for the local drug store in this small Alabama town and he had come to the post office to deliver a package to the sergeant.

"How much is it, boy?" The sergeant barked at this nervous messenger.

"The price is on the package, sir," Jeff answered.

"I know that, boy. But that wasn't my question. Are you so dumb that you can't read? Well, can you read or not?"

Jeff was getting even more nervous, standing before this well-groomed, smartly-uniformed soldier.

"I asked you a question, boy. Can you read?"

"Yes, sir. I can read," Jeff replied.

"Then read what it says on the package," the sergeant demanded.

"Seventy-five cents," Jeff mumbled.

"Read the whole goddamn thing," the sergeant shouted, "every word. Read it loud and clear."

"Sergeant James Kirkland, United States Post Office," Jeff read nervously.

"That's better, boy. Speak up. I don't have time to waste on your kind."

Sergeant Faulkner threw three quarters at Jeff. As Jeff turned to leave, the sergeant looked at the skinny black boy. "Turn around, boy. Look at me. Look me in the eyes. Stand up straight."

Jeff was suspicious of this man in uniform and he just wanted to leave. But there was something about the sergeant's demeanor that caused him to obey. Sergeant Faulkner's demeanor seemed to soften as he looked at the boy, head to toe. He smiled. "You look healthy, boy. How'd you like to join the United States Army? Maybe we could put a few pounds on that skinny frame."

Jeff was now becoming very agitated and he wanted to get out of the presence of this moody Army man.

"Well," the sergeant said, "do we have a deal? Can I sign you up? Your life'll be a lot better if you're in the Army. Besides, your country's at war and every able-bodied boy has a duty to serve."

Jeff stood before this tall soldier, trying to make sense of what was being said.

"Now, you know you have to be eighteen years old and have your parents' permission to join the Army, don't you? How old are you, boy?"

"I'm eighteen, sir," Jeff replied.

"All right," the sergeant said, "tomorrow, bring your parents here. We'll get their signatures or their marks, if they can't write."

Jeff's brains were spinning in his head. He knew he had just lied to the sergeant and he saw himself being victimized by his own lie. Although he had just lied about his age, the thought of joining the Army and wearing a smart uniform such as the one the sergeant wore excited him. After all, he reasoned, his lie was for a good cause.

"Sergeant," Jeff spoke up, "I can't bring my parents here. They work. They'll lose their jobs if they miss a day."

The sergeant sighed, "All right. If I give you the enlistment papers, can I trust you to get them signed and bring them back to me?"

"Yes, sir," Jeff said. "You can trust me."

With papers in hand, Jeff left the post office and headed back to work. He tried to make sense of the rapid developments swirling around him. Did he really look eighteen? Or was the recruiting officer trying to set a trap for him that would cause him trouble?

That night, Jeff hid the enlistment papers under the mattress of the bed where he slept with his younger brother. All night, he lay awake, trying to sort this whole mess out. At dawn, he knew what he had to do. He would take a chance, sign the papers himself and return them to the sergeant. Jeff suddenly felt empowered. This worldly sergeant believed that he was eighteen. He wanted him for the Army.

"Hell," Jeff reasoned, "I'm not going to back down."

On a Thursday morning in 1942, Jeff returned the enlistment papers to Sergeant Faulkner at the recruiting office. The sergeant quietly and slowly examined the papers. Jeff had forged the signatures of his mother and his father.

Sergeant Faulkner looked up at Jeff with a stern face and piercing eyes. Suddenly, Jeff was terrified. Did the sergeant see through his deceit? Was he going to call the police and have him locked up because he had forged a government document? Jeff wanted to turn and run out of the office. But he stood fast. Finally, after what seemed like ages, Sergeant Faulkner looked up and smiled.

"Okay, boy," the sergeant said. "I'll pick you up at six A.M. on Monday and get you over to Fort Benning, Georgia, for a physical. If you pass, you'll be sworn in and sent for basic training. I'll pick you up and get you to the bus station. Now that you're going to become a soldier we demand that you be prompt," the sergeant ordered.

Jeff's pulse quickened. How could he allow the sergeant to pick him up at home when his mother and father knew nothing about this grand scheme?

"Sergeant," Jeff said hastily, "I probably won't sleep much over the weekend, so I'll be up and at the bus station by five thirty A.M."

"You'd best be there, boy," Sergeant Faulkner replied. "The Army waits for no one."

Friday, Saturday, and Sunday were very anxious days. Jeff had lied to Sergeant Faulkner about his age and now he was about to run away from home. What would this do to his family, especially to his mother? Jeff knew it was too late to back out now. He risked prosecution if the Army found out that his papers were forged. If he stayed at home, he had only poverty, racial discrimination and

abuse ahead of him. He would take the chance and meet Sergeant
Faulkner.

Jeff suddenly remembered that his mother often spoke of how
she looked forward to the time when her children would be old
enough to leave Alabama and the South to go to a place where
they could find better opportunities for an education and jobs.
Maybe she would see his running away as the fulfillment of her
dreams for him. He had fooled Sergeant Faulkner into believing he
was eighteen, but would the doctors at Fort Benning see through
his big lie? He was at the point of no return. He knew that he
faced damnation, no matter what he did. To Jeff, no matter what
happened, it couldn't be much worse than his present
circumstances.

He was still shaken by his memory of the night the Ku Klux
Klan came to hang his father. The sight of that burning cross was
seared into his brain. The Klan was never very far from the minds
of black folk, especially those living in the South. The Klan was a
terrorist organization. Its members took great pride in being able
to rule by using terror as their chief weapon. To Jeff and other
blacks, it was not just the threat of Klan terror that was so
frightening; it was the knowledge that the Klan's threats almost
always led to great physical pain and death.

Lying in bed next to his younger brother, Jeff's whole life started
to flash before his eyes. He wanted desperately to fall asleep but
the excitement of what he was about to do prevented sleep from
overtaking his consciousness. Jeff knew very well that it was wrong
to lie, but he also knew that he and his family had been forced to
lie on more occasions than he could remember. Each day when he
reported for work at the drug store, he was forced by fear to say he
felt good, even when his stomach was in pain because of lack of
food. Mr. Grady would slap him on the back and say, "How you
doin', boy?" And he would smile and reply, "I feel good, Mr. Grady,
real good." Most times that was a lie. But he knew that if he revealed
his true feelings, he would put his job at risk. His family could ill
afford to lose the three dollars a week he took home to help them
survive.

He lied when he was asked what he wanted to be when he grew up. In an effort to avoid being called uppity, he would say that he liked being a delivery boy, when, in fact, he hated not having the opportunity to attend school like the white children his age.

As he lay awake in this dark room listening to the breathing of his sleeping younger brother, he thought, "What other decision was there?" Was the lie he told about his age any different from the lies he had been forced to tell for most of his life? Wasn't there such a thing as a good lie to get out of a very bad situation? Sergeant Faulkner had said that the country was at war and every able-bodied boy was needed. Perhaps the needs of the country outweighed the lie Jeff had told about his age. Maybe there was such a thing as a justifiable lie. If so, maybe it was justifiable to lie in order to escape a deplorable situation that seemed to have no end. Maybe it was justifiable when one was in search of a life with purpose and meaning. No matter what, the lie was told and Jeff believed, he truly believed, that the consequences of being caught in his lie could not be any more severe than the consequences of the life he had been forced to live so far.

Wild thoughts and ideas swept through Jeff's brain as he tried, without success, to fall into the only thing that he really craved, sleep. But sleep would not come. The thoughts and ideas kept coming. Suppose this scheme really worked. Suppose those at Fort Benning believed, as Sergeant Faulkner believed, that he was eighteen. Suppose he became a soldier? What would that mean? Would it mean better treatment? Would there be an opportunity for him to learn to read better and to speak better? Was it possible that he would have the chance to verbalize what he really felt without fear of being physically abused or even killed?

Just before daybreak, Jeff had come to the conclusion that he would go through with his scheme. He would leave home, run away and enlist in the United States Army. Grandma Dawson had often said that for "colored" people, life is a series of chances; that you had to pick your best chance and pursue it with all your might. Jeff reasoned that this was his best chance and he had to go forward with it. This rare opportunity might never come again.

When he sneaked out of bed that morning, his younger brother was sleeping soundly. Jeff walked down the hallway, past his mother and father's room. He was tempted to knock on the door and tell them he was leaving, but he knew that this wouldn't work. His parents would never allow him to leave home. What would the sergeant do if he failed to show up? Jeff was filled with all kinds of emotions as he eased the front door open and headed for the bus station.

His last, nagging thought was of the money his family would lose when he left home. At the drug store where he worked, he was paid three dollars a week for six and a half days' work. Jeff kept fifty cents from his weekly pay and he gave the remaining two and a half dollars to his mother. Mama Essie would miss him greatly, but she would also miss the contribution he made to the family. Perhaps he could find a way to send money to her from his Army pay of twenty-one dollars a month. He would try to find a way.

When he was out of the black section of town, Jeff felt a sense of relief. He had been afraid that he would be seen by someone who knew him and that they would ask why he was out before daybreak. If this happened, his whole plan could fall apart. Certainly there would be talk about him being missing. Everyone in this small town knew everyone else. He wanted to leave no clue that could possibly lead to the discovery of his whereabouts. As he left the black section of town, he began to breathe a little easier.

Jeff was four blocks from the bus station, in the white section of town, when a police squad car suddenly pulled out of a driveway. The police officer ordered him to stop. Jeff was almost paralyzed with fear. He knew that there was a penalty for a black person, especially a black male, who was caught walking in a white neighborhood at night. It was not night, but it was barely daybreak. Jeff was certain that all of his plans would now start to unravel. The police might even subject him to a beating before he was thrown into the city jail.

The burly policeman stepped out of the squad car and approached Jeff, all the while shining his flashlight directly into Jeff's eyes. "What's your name, boy?"

"My name's Jeff, sir."

"What are you doin' in this section of town at this time of day, boy?"

"I'm on my way to the bus station, sir."

"Ain't no bus leaving here 'til eight thirty. That's almost three hours from now. I don't like smart niggers lyin' to me."

"I'm not lying to you, sir. I have to meet Sergeant Faulkner and take a bus to Fort Benning, Georgia."

"You going to join the Army, boy?"

"Yes, sir. I'm going to join the Army," Jeff said.

"Aw right. Go on down to the bus depot. I'm gonna check on you. If I find that you lied to me, you're gonna be a sorry nigger. Now you get on down to the bus depot before I decide to lock you up!"

Jeff assumed a very brisk pace to get out of the presence of the policeman. He arrived at the bus station at a little past five o'clock on Monday morning. It was very bleak and rainy. The January weather sent chills through his skinny frame. A feeling of terror seized him. Here he was about to leave the place he had known for all of his young life. Except for the time he went to Columbia, Alabama to visit his grandmother on his father's side, Jeff had never been more than three or four miles from home. Now, on this day, he was about to board a bus and ride away to a place that was totally foreign to him. It was not so much that he was leaving this place. It was the manner in which he was leaving. He loved his family very much and he wished, desperately, that he could say goodbye to them.

When he arrived at the bus station, Sergeant Faulkner was already there. "Go on inside and have a seat," he told Jeff. "The bus will be here in twenty minutes."

At the bus station were twenty-five or thirty men. The station was alive with conversations between wives, mothers and fathers who had come to see their husbands and sons off to war. Jeff walked into the "colored" waiting room and took a seat. Tears filled his eyes now as it became painfully clear to him that he was alone—all alone—and that his life would never again be the same. The "colored" section of the bus station was empty. Jeff was relieved to see this, because everyone in this little town knew each other. Had there been one person in the "colored" section of the station, his secret would have been revealed. Someone would have told his family that he had run away and joined the Army.

As Jeff entered the "colored" waiting room, he saw the policeman he had encountered earlier. The officer came into the waiting room and stood directly over Jeff, who was now seated on the front row of wooden seats. "Glad to see you weren't lyin' to me, boy. I hate lyin' niggers."

Jeff looked up at the policeman but he said nothing. As the policeman paced back and forth, slapping his nightstick into his open palm, Sergeant Faulkner entered the "colored" waiting room.

"Is there something wrong here?" the sergeant demanded.

"I ain't sure," the policeman replied. "I caught this nigger boy walkin' down the street. He claims he's gonna join the Army. I'm just checkin' on him. You know how some of them lie."

Sergeant Faulkner's reply was crisp and to the point. "He's not lying. His papers are signed and in order. In a few hours, he'll be sworn into the United States Army."

As Sergeant Faulkner was speaking to the policeman, the bus that would take the enlistees to Fort Benning pulled into the station. The sergeant turned his attention from the policeman and spoke directly to Jeff.

"Wiggins," he said, "you're in my care. You don't have to be afraid of anything or anyone, except me. As long as you do exactly what I tell you, you don't even have to be afraid of me. Do you understand?"

"I understand you, Sergeant."

With that, the sergeant ushered the policeman out of the waiting room. The sergeant turned, winked at Jeff and gave him a "thumbs up" sign.

"Glad to see you made it, boy. Just wait here. I'll let you know when it's time to board the bus."

CHAPTER TWO

After the twenty-eight white enlistees had boarded the bus, Sergeant Faulkner came into the "colored" waiting room and spoke to Jeff. "All right, boy. You can get on the bus now—the back seat is empty. You'll sit there."

As Jeff walked down the long aisle of the Greyhound bus, he was aware that stares were directed at him. One white enlistee shouted to the others on the bus, "Hey, fellows, look! We got a 'coon' who wants to be a soldier!"

Sergeant Faulkner looked sharply in the direction of the man. "Shut your goddamn mouth. The Germans and the Japanese don't give a shit whether you're a 'coon' or a 'redneck'. And they won't hesitate to blow your fuckin' brains out!"

While he was seated on the long back seat of the Greyhound bus for the two-hour trip to Fort Benning, Georgia, Jeff's mind started to wander. He took offense at being ridiculed and called a "coon", but bitter past experience had taught him that it was futile to react. While some of the white enlistees on the bus may also have been offended at the "coon" remark, Jeff knew that none would speak up and risk being called a "nigger lover". Whites in the South of 1942 knew what was expected of them. There were boundaries for both races and crossing those invisible boundaries almost always led to violence.

The bus finally left the station and turned onto Highway 231 in the direction of Georgia. What was Jeff leaving and what was in his future? He knew at this moment he was truly alone in the world. He could not write home and he could not talk to anyone about what he had done. Had he made a good decision or had he messed up his life to the extent that it could never be repaired? Whatever the answer, there was no turning back.

The motion of the Greyhound bus combined with his lack of sleep the night before made him drowsy, but Jeff tried to fight off sleep because he needed to think. By now, he knew that his whole family would be up and getting ready for work or for school. What would they think when they found him missing? No one in his family had ever run away and Jeff felt sad that he was the first. He knew that his mother would comb the neighborhood looking for him. Perhaps she would go to the police and they would find out that he had lied and forged his parents' signatures to get into the Army. All of these wild thoughts shot through his mind as the bus rolled along the highway. As hard as he fought it, sleep overtook him.

Was he dreaming or was he reliving an event that he had tried over the years to forget? It had been a few years now since the Ku Klux Klan had come in the middle of the night. It all came back to him now. In his mind, he was that six-year-old boy living in the shack on the edge of the dense woods. They had been sleeping soundly that night—his whole family. For the first time in days, they had gone to bed with full stomachs. His father, Clem, had sold a bale of cotton and bought food for his family of eleven people—mother and father, seven children, grandmother and aunt. His father had demanded that they go to bed early, because the next day would be a long, hard day. There were still several bales of cotton to be picked before the rains came.

Suddenly, in what seemed like a dream, the whole family awoke to much commotion. All seven children jumped out of bed and flung open the wooden shutters that served as window coverings. There, in the middle of their yard, stood a huge burning cross, surrounded by a dozen or more Klansmen in full regalia.

Jeff was too young to internalize what this meant for the family, especially what it meant for his father, Clem. He could, however, appreciate the drama that this scene held—the huge cross burning with what seemed like great anger; the men in hooded white robes and headgear that prevented the viewer from seeing their faces; restless horses prancing in the background; the glare from the shotguns, plainly visible. One man had what looked to Jeff like a new rope. Jeff could not fully understand the drama unfolding around him, but he knew that this was something special.

Were these real men and real horses or was this some kind of punishment visited upon them by a power greater than themselves? On many occasions, he had heard Grandma Dawson talk about "reaping what you sow". At times, his mother, Mama Essie, spoke very passionately of haints or ghosts. It seemed that haints or ghosts always came at midnight and were always dressed in white. They appeared to have supernatural powers. They disappeared when you tried to touch them. Maybe these strange figures were haints or maybe this was the apocalypse he had once heard the preacher talk about. Whatever it was, Jeff knew it was serious and it frightened him.

It was his Grandma Dawson's terror-filled voice shouting, "It's the Klan!" that brought Jeff back to reality. He and his brothers closed the wooden shutters and ran to be near Mama Essie and Grandma Dawson.

"I'll do the talking," Grandma Dawson said in a stern voice. "Everybody else keep your mouths closed."

A feeling of great panic gripped the whole family. Why had the Klan come here? What had they done?

The Klan leader left the group, accompanied by three other Klansmen, and approached the front door. Grandma Dawson, clad in a long flannel nightgown, stepped out on the front porch to meet them. If she was afraid, she did not show it.

"Where's that nigger, Clem?" the leader demanded.

"I don't know where the nigger is," Grandma Dawson replied. "I've been looking for him, too. If I find him, he's a dead nigger."

The Klansman's response was more an order than a question. "If he comes back, will you let us know?"

"Yes, sir, but only after I kill him!" she said, almost in a whisper. "If you think I'm lying, sir, you're welcome to search the house."

"I believe you," the leader said angrily.

With that, he returned to the larger group. They mounted their horses and rode away, leaving the huge cross still burning brightly.

Grandma Dawson's father had been born into slavery and she knew how to perform in the presence of the whites. She always said what she knew they wanted to hear. Among the white people of the farming community, she was looked upon as a good, loyal, responsible old nigger woman. Among blacks in the same community, Grandma Dawson was seen as a survivalist. She had, on many occasions, helped black men to leave the South when they were suspected of betraying the trust of whites.

After the Klan had left, Grandma Dawson instructed the family to sit down around the long kitchen table. She told them that she, Mama Essie, and Jeff's father, Clem, had been on the alert for the Klan and had heard the horses approaching. Moments before they arrived, Clem had left through the window in the back and escaped into the woods.

"Why did the Klan want to kill Daddy?" Jeff asked timidly. He could barely say the word "kill" because it noted such finality.

Grandma Dawson spoke to all of them. "Now, you listen to me and be sure you hear every word I say. Your father risked his life to put food on the table where you're now sitting. He's a good man, a hero. He sold a bale of cotton without the boss man's permission because we hadn't eaten in three or four days. Hold up your heads. Be proud of your daddy." Grandma Dawson continued, "The Good Book says 'greater is the love of no man if he is willing to give his life for his friends'. Your friend, your daddy, loves all of us and now he's wandering out there in the woods, scared to come home. God bless you, Clem. We're safe for now. Our stomachs are full. Our faith is strong. And we love you because you sacrificed for us."

After Grandma Dawson finished talking, she ordered Sonny Boy and Pinkie, the oldest boy and girl, to go out into the yard to knock down the burning cross. She told them to draw water from the well to put the fire out. Mama Essie and Aunt Mae began packing the family's meager belongings for the move from the farm to the nearest town, seven or eight miles away.

The excitement and the drama of the events that had unfolded less than an hour before had been too much for Jeff to comprehend.

Just before sunrise, the fully loaded wagon, pulled by two mules, came to a stop in front of Uncle Eddie's house. Uncle Eddie, Mama Essie's brother, had no room for this new brood, but he fully understood what had taken place out on the farm and he took the family in with open arms.

"Some of ya'll have to sleep on the floor," he said, "but at least you'll have a roof over your heads. We'll do the best we can about eating."

After the family had unloaded the wagon and put the mules in the small stable in the back of the house, Jeff asked Mama Essie, "What about Daddy? How will he know where we are?"

"Don't worry about your daddy, son. He's safe and he'll find us. Just leave this whole matter in the hands of the Lord."

In spite of the fear and the terror that caused his family to have to move from the farm to the small town, Jeff and his brothers felt a sense of relief. The family had always lived on a farm and life in a city was something they thought they would never experience.

A week after the Klan incident, Jeff's father came to Uncle Eddie's house in the middle of the night. Jeff and his brothers would have slept through his arrival but the sound of Grandma Dawson making a fire in the kitchen stove woke them up. Jeff wasn't quite certain what he should do but he moved hesitantly from the pallet on the hard floor and entered the kitchen. For the first time in a week, he came face to face with his daddy.

"Daddy, how do you feel?" Jeff said.

"I'm all right, boy," his father replied. "I need a strong cup of coffee and a bath and I'll be good as new."

"Sit your behind down, Clem," Mama Dawson ordered. "You can have your coffee and a bath as soon as this stove heats up."

Jeff could hardly take his eyes off his father. He had a frightened look about him and he had appeared to have lost some weight. Looking at his father and trying to imagine what he had been through caused a feeling of anger to surge through Jeff's entire body. He now realized the great courage that had been required for his father to save his family from starvation.

Sitting at the kitchen table, Jeff's father seemed small and very lonely. His eyes seemed to look deep into the past and into an uncertain future at the same time. Sweat poured from his father's deep black skin. Mama Essie kept wiping his face, but the sweat continued to pour from his brow.

Grandma Dawson tapped Jeff on the shoulder, "Boy, you go on back in the room and get some sleep. There's nothing you can do here."

"No," his father snapped, "let him stay. Maybe he can learn a lesson here."

"What kind of lesson can he learn?" Grandma Dawson replied. "He's just a boy."

"He can learn what fear and terror these white folks spread to keep things the way they are now," his father whispered. "I'm too old to change the way whites and blacks see each other. But maybe, with a little luck, he can use this experience to try to change things. It's too late for me but it's not too late for him. Remember what you see here boy," his father said.

CHAPTER THREE

At Eufala, Alabama, the bus came to a stop. Sergeant Faulkner announced that there was just enough time to get a cup of coffee and use the bathroom. On the side of the road, there was a small café with a white lettered sign on a black background. The sign read, "Whites Only". As the white enlistees filed into the small café, Jeff remained seated. He was aware that he would not be allowed in the café. The sergeant came to the back of the bus. "What's wrong, boy? Don't you want a cup of coffee? Do you have to use the bathroom?"

"I do," Jeff replied. "But I can't go in there. It's for whites only."

"Aw, shit," Faulkner said. "Go around to the back of the building and relieve yourself. I'll see if I can bring you a cup of coffee out here."

Minutes later, the sergeant entered the bus, carrying a paper container that held steaming hot coffee. Sergeant Faulkner turned his head as he handed the hot coffee to Jeff.

"Thank you," Jeff said.

"Don't be so goddamned polite. I shouldn't have to do this. You're about to become a soldier and risk your life for these people. What in hell do you have to be thankful for, boy?"

Jeff just stared at the sergeant. He had no reply. What could he say?

The sergeant ordered everyone back on the bus. The final leg of the trip to Fort Benning would take a little more than an hour. As the bus rolled along, the feeling of being lost and helpless returned. Jeff had been able to sell the big lie about his age to Sergeant Faulkner, but soon he would have to stand before a battery of skilled Army doctors. Would they, too, believe that he was just a tall, skinny, undernourished farm boy? Or would they see him for what he really was—a child trying to be a man? Did his voice sound manly or would it betray him and cause him to be placed on a bus back home?

The worst scenario that came to Jeff's mind was being thrown in jail and being put on trial for lying to Army officials. The pressure of the deceit he had perpetrated and the colossal lie he had told to the Army, the possibility that his whole scheme could unravel in just a few hours—all of these thoughts and feelings evoked painful, converging emotions that threw Jeff into a frenzy that was almost paralyzing. It was at this time that Jeff began to recall some of the things his mother had said to her children, especially her boys.

Mama Essie would always gather them around her during times of trouble. She would say, "It's hard to be a man in a world where the odds are against you. But you have to find a way to overcome the odds and move forward. The very people who have been oppressing you don't realize it, but they have really been oppressing themselves. You can't keep a man down in a ditch unless you get down in the ditch and hold him there. One day, the man who's holding you down will have to get up. And when he does, you, too, will be able to get up and step out of the ditch. When that happens, I want you to be ready. I want you to be free."

Was this what Mama Essie was talking about? Had Sergeant Faulkner inadvertently removed himself from the ditch and, in doing so, had he allowed Jeff to get out, too? Was the United States Army a first step on the long road to freedom? No matter what the consequences, the die was cast and Jeff knew that what he had set in motion could not be brought to a halt just because he was almost overcome with fear.

Finally, the Greyhound bus rolled to a stop in front of the reception center at Fort Benning, Georgia. Sergeant Faulkner was the first to exit. Outside, Jeff could see several soldiers, smartly uniformed and looking very stern. After a brief exchange of words, Faulkner handed over a roster to the sergeant who was in charge of the incoming enlistees. Two sergeants and two corporals entered the bus. They looked and acted as if they were extremely angry.

One sergeant shouted, "When I say 'move', every one of you sorry, miserable-looking recruits better get your asses off this bus before I can blink my eyes! Move!"

A mad scramble to get off the bus was in full swing. From his seat in the back of the bus, Jeff also started scrambling to exit. Just as he was about to step off the bus, the sergeant quickly seized his arm.

"Where the hell do you think you're goin', boy?" The look in the sergeant's eyes froze Jeff in his tracks.

"I . . ."

"Who the hell told you to speak, boy? You speak only when I tell you to speak. Do you read me, boy?"

"Yes, sir."

"Who told you to say 'yes, sir'? Did I give you permission to speak?" Now, Jeff was thoroughly confused. To speak or not to speak? Welcome to the United States Army.

When he was off the bus and on the ground, the sergeant called a corporal who was standing nearby and shouted, "Get this miserable man out of my face. I don't care what you do with him, but get him away from me!"

One word in the sergeant's tirade struck Jeff's brain like a thunderbolt. He had called him a "man". This was the first time in his life that anyone had ever referred to him as a "man". Maybe this Army wasn't so bad after all. Had the sergeant seen something in Jeff that no one else had ever recognized?

The corporal led Jeff to a building filled with other enlistees and draftees, all of them black. He was seated next to a man in his early thirties, or so Jeff guessed. The man looked at Jeff and said, "What the hell are you doin' here? You look like you haven't been weaned from your mama's breast."

Before he could reply, someone from the medical department ordered everyone to strip and file into the examining rooms. As he was going from one doctor to the next, Jeff wondered if some doctor would see him in the same manner as the man he was seated next to had seen him.

The physicals were quick but thorough. The doctors asked Jeff several questions about his health history, but none seemed to find

reason to question his age. At the last station, he was given a series
of injections that certified he had passed the physical and could
now be sworn in as a soldier in the United States Army.

A sense of relief surged through Jeff now that he had passed
his physical and was a real soldier. As Jeff moved through the line
at the supply room where the soldiers were measured and fitted
for uniforms, the supply sergeant had difficulty finding a uniform
that fit him properly. The length of the trousers was fine, but
there was nothing in stock that would fit his waistline. The olive
drab jacket hung off his frame like that of a Halloween skeleton.

"You better eat six times a day, soldier, to get some flesh on
that skinny frame of yours," the supply sergeant bellowed.

Back in the barracks, there were a few hours of downtime before
it was time to go to classification, where each soldier would learn
where he would be sent for basic training. Most of his fellow soldiers
used the time to write letters home, but Jeff sat on his bunk in
deep thought. He could not write home, or anywhere else, for that
matter. He could not afford to reveal his whereabouts, because to
do so would cause his new world—his world of manhood in the
United States Army—to come tumbling down. Now, more than
at any time since he had run away from home, he felt truly alone.

During the time when he was growing up, he had heard
Grandma Dawson speak about God banishing Moses to the back
of the mountain. Jeff didn't need to imagine how Moses felt. He
knew. He knew, not because God had banished him; he had
banished himself. As he sat there on the bunk, he glanced at the
clock. It was now 5:17 P.M. He had been gone for a whole day.
Mama Essie always made breakfast for him and she made certain
that he looked presentable before he left for his job at the drug
store. What had she thought that morning when she came into
the room where he and his brother slept and found him gone? He
had never before left home without telling her where he was going.
It would never occur to her that he had run away. Mama Essie
probably thought that Mr. Grady, the storeowner, had told him
to come in a little early and that Jeff did not want to wake her that
early. But what would it be like when he did not come home at

night? Would she think the worst? What would his brothers and sisters think?

January 13, 1942 was a milestone in Jeff's life. It was not only the day he ran away from home, but it was also the day he became a man. Had not the sergeant told the corporal to take "this man" away? Even now, when it was time to fall in for a march to the mess hall or to numerous orientation sessions, the order was always, "Fall in, men."

This was very important to Jeff. Throughout his short life, it was as if he had no name except at home. At the drug store, at delivery stops, it was almost always the same. "Come here, boy," "Do this, boy," or, "Hurry up, boy." Somehow, the term "man" seemed softer, more humane, and more respectful.

As he thought about it today, he was not alone in being referred to as "boy". If you were black in the South, no matter what your age, you were a "boy". In some instances, some more moderate whites—and they were few—would refer to the more senior blacks as "preacher", "auntie" or "uncle". You never became a man or woman and "Mr." or "Mrs." was out of the question.

Today, Jeff was in a brand-new world. He was a soldier. But, more important, he was a man, a man recognized by no less an entity than the United States of America. How much better did it get? After five days at Fort Benning, doing all of the things new recruits are required to do, Jeff and seventy-two other soldiers were shipped off to Fort Bragg, North Carolina for eight weeks of basic training.

CHAPTER FOUR

On the train headed for Fort Bragg, Jeff was again alone in his thoughts. He could not write home, nor could he have contact with any of his lifelong friends. He worried about his family and he knew that they must be crazy to know his whereabouts. At the drug store, he earned three dollars a week. With the exception of one-half dollar, he willingly turned his money over to his mother. Mama Essie earned a few dollars as a stay-at-home dressmaker. With Jeff's earnings and her own, along with what Jeff's older sister earned as a maid, his mother bought food and paid the rent. When she could, she bought second-hand shoes and clothes for the children. Now the part of Mama Essie's income that Jeff had provided was lost. How would this affect her ability to keep the family together?

Jeff's pay as an army private was twenty-one dollars a month. He wanted desperately to send his entire pay home to Mama Essie, but he could not do this without risking having his whole world fall down around him. There was talk in the barracks that a private's pay would soon be increased to the unheard-of amount of fifty dollars a month. If this proved to be true, he would simply have to find a way to send money home.

The eight weeks of basic training at Fort Bragg, North Carolina were difficult and stressful. Jeff learned to have confidence in himself and to obey orders without the thought of questioning why. He was very good at close-order drill and he very quickly learned the nomenclature of the weapons. He learned about the thirty-caliber rifle and the 155-mm howitzer. Aside from his weapons expertise, Jeff's most valuable assets were his memory and his ability to follow instructions. He could recite, almost verbatim, every Army regulation read to him and those he read himself. At the conclusion of basic training, Jeff had been classified as suitable for further training to become a military policeman.

With basic training behind him, Jeff was a little anxious and depressed. Over the past eight weeks, he had been kept extremely busy from six in the morning until ten at night. But now he had a little more time to reflect upon the thing that mattered most—his family.

Indeed, the military did raise the pay for privates from twenty-one to fifty dollars a month, with added incentives for married soldiers and for those who had dependents. With this much money, he could do a lot for his family. But he did not dare even undertake the simple task of writing them a letter. Jeff knew that Mama Essie could use the money, but he also knew that she would never give up her underage son to the Army, no matter what amount of money she was offered.

The pressure continued to plague Jeff. No matter where he went or what he did, the question on his mind was always the same, "How can I help my family and still remain a soldier?" He liked the Army. It gave him the dignity and the respect that he could never get in southern Alabama in 1942. There must be a way out of this dilemma. He had to find that way.

CHAPTER FIVE

After completing basic training, Jeff was on the move again. This time, he traveled north. Fort Wadsworth on Staten Island, New York became his new Army home. Before enlisting in the Army, he had never been more than a few miles from home. Funny, but he could now recall the month he had spent with his Grandma Patience in Columbia, Alabama. His father had put him on the train for the eleven-mile trip. The train stopped in Columbia, but there was no one there to meet him. It was about ten o'clock on Sunday night and it was very dark in this godforsaken country. Jeff stood on the side of the tracks, in the dark, scared out of his wits. He wondered why no one had come to meet him. He knew that Grandma Patience lived about three or four miles up the road from the train stop, so he started to walk toward her house. Maybe he would meet her on the way.

After walking more than a mile, he met no one, but he thought he heard strange voices and he could swear he saw ghost-like figures dancing in the distance. Each time he stopped to take a closer look, there was nothing there. He was only about ten years old and he had already heard a thousand stories about the ghosts or haints that came out late at night. As soon as he started to walk again, these ghost-like figures appeared—or so he thought.

When he was within a mile of Grandma Patience's house, he saw a small church and he knew there had to be a cemetery there. He tried not to look, but, sure enough, he saw the small cemetery right next to the church building.

Most of the family on Jeff's father's side was buried in that small cemetery. After seeing it, he ran the rest of the way to Grandma Patience's house. Upon his arrival, Jeff was out of breath. In addition, he was very disappointed that no one had met him at the train stop and accompanied him on that frightening walk. However, he dared not ask why he had been left alone. He just said, "I'm glad to see you, Grandma."

Her reply was not exactly sympathetic or comforting. "What took you so long to get here?"

Grandma Patience was Jeff's grandmother on his father's side. Everyone knew she had a very mean streak in her. Neither Jeff, nor any of his sisters or brothers could ever remember seeing Grandma Patience smile. Most people were afraid of her. She did not seem to know that there was such a thing as civility. If you greeted her, she just stared at you and her staring sent chills through your spine.

Jeff could remember once asking Grandma Patience how she felt, only to receive the patented stare, accompanied by the words, "How the hell do you think I feel, you mannish little good-for-nothing bastard?" In spite of her attitude, Jeff somehow still sincerely believed that Grandma Patience loved him dearly.

CHAPTER SIX

Jeff's new station at Fort Wadsworth was a long, long way from his beginnings. He was in awe of the big city and all of the hustle and bustle around him. In his wildest dreams, he had never imagined that he would see a place like New York. Unfortunately, there was precious little time to take in the magic of the city. Training to become a military policeman kept him busy from early morning until late evening. In spite of his hard work, at the conclusion of the twelve weeks of training, Jeff was assigned to the duty of company clerk. He was disappointed that he was not assigned to patrol duty in the city, but he was very disciplined and he would never allow his disappointment to show.

His duties as a company clerk did give him great insight into how the Army operated, at least at the company level. Jeff had access to the records of all two hundred and forty-eight men in his company. He had direct access to the first sergeant—the most powerful enlisted man in the company. The officers of the company frequently called upon Jeff to give them information about certain individual soldiers. He knew that the captain, the company commander, liked his work ethic and his devotion to duty. Jeff knew all of these things because the captain had said to him, "Stay on course, soldier. There's a future in this man's Army for people like you."

For the first time in his life, someone had told him he had a future. This captain had validated, in a way that he would never know, that Jeff's hopes and dreams "to be somebody" could, in time, become a reality. From that day on, Jeff vowed that he would be a model soldier. He was first in all things—first in formations, first in knowledge about the affairs of the Army and first to anticipate the needs of the first sergeant, the captain and all of the other company officers. In his off-duty time, he read everything he could get his hands on—*The New York Times, The Daily News, The Pittsburgh Courier* and all manner of military rules and regulations.

He had only been to New York City twice in his nine months at Fort Wadsworth. He once went to Times Square, just to look. Another time he went up to 125th Street to see a part of Harlem. On the corner of 125th Street and 8th Avenue, he bought two Nedick's hotdogs and a large orange soda. The bulk of his money was locked away in his footlocker. Jeff had saved the grand sum of four hundred and fifty dollars. Someday, he told himself, he would find a way to get all of the money he had saved to his mother. A song that Mama Essie frequently sang was always on his mind. "I know the Lord will make a way somehow."

Jeff kept telling himself, "He will."

CHAPTER SEVEN

On his birthday, February 22, Jeff was promoted to sergeant. Maybe the captain was right. Maybe he did have a future in this man's Army. If he was going to continue to advance toward a brighter future, in the Army or anywhere else, Jeff knew that he had to learn a lot more than he knew at that time. His formal education had been a hit-and-miss affair, at best. He had only been able to go to school part time. The other part of his life was spent working as a delivery boy for a local drug store and doing odd jobs to help his family keep their collective head above water. It took lots and lots of food to feed seven growing children.

At best, Jeff had a fifth or sixth grade education. He could read well. His mother had taught him and his sisters and brothers to read the Bible. Mama Essie also read the Bible to them.

Jeff's imagination always seemed to run wild. When Mama Essie read from the New Testament, he could see John the Baptist baptizing Jesus in the Sea of Galilee. He could see Jesus as He preached the sermon on the mountain. But he knew that he needed more.

One day, in an informal talk with one of the company officers, a first lieutenant, Jeff asked, "Sir, if you wanted to find a source of great knowledge, where would you go?"

The lieutenant answered matter of factly, "To the library, Sergeant, to the library." Jeff had never seen the inside of a library. There was a library in his hometown, but it was for whites only.

A week later, Jeff found himself in the library in Stapleton, Staten Island, New York. He was in awe of what he saw—shelves and shelves of books. He was like a child on his first visit to the circus. He wanted to see and examine every book.

After a while, he had touched almost every bookshelf in the

library. A very kind librarian approached him.

"My name is Mrs. Merrill," she announced. "Are you looking for a special kind of book?"

"Yes, ma'am, I'm looking for a book of great knowledge," Jeff stated.

"Does this book have a title?" Mrs. Merrill asked quizzically.

"I don't know, ma'am. I just know that I need to learn a lot more than I know now."

"I can issue you a library card. When you find that book of great knowledge you can check it out."

She started to walk away when Jeff looked into her eyes, pleadingly, and said, "You don't understand. I've never been inside a library before and I don't know what I'm looking for. Help me, please."

Mrs. Merrill walked to the circulation desk. She told the desk attendant that she would be busy with a soldier for a while and she was not to be disturbed. Mrs. Merrill took a complete inventory of where Jeff had been, where he wanted to go and what he wanted to be. Over the next four months, she introduced him to many books and articles, including *Up from Slavery*, books by Booker T. Washington, W.E.B. DuBois and Frederick Douglass, as well as the works of Langston Hughes.

"These books," Mrs. Merrill said, "will let you know that you are somebody."

Next, she brought out the works of John Locke, Thomas Jefferson, and the Federalist papers. Over the months, Jeff began to understand more about his own race and the philosophy of the founding fathers. Mostly he learned that only you can define who you are and where you want to go. He would always remember this and he would always say a special prayer for Mrs. Merrill. She, as much as anyone, had removed the veil of ignorance that had blinded him.

CHAPTER EIGHT

"Sergeant, notify the platoon sergeant that there will be a reading of the Articles of War in the company day room at o-nine hundred hours tomorrow," First Sergeant Thomas said to Jeff. Every soldier thought that this activity was a waste of time. But commanders were required by regulation to read these articles to the troops at least once every six months.

The Articles of War defined the code of conduct for all military personnel. Jeff had heard it read at least four or five times and he was resigned to listen to it again. The monotone of today's reader was enough to put every soldier in the room to sleep. The second lieutenant recognized that most of the troops were drowsy. A few had fallen asleep.

"Take a five-minute break," the lieutenant announced, "and we'll continue after the break."

When the reading resumed, the first article hit Jeff like Joe Louis punching a heavy bag. The article stated that whoever enlists into the Army with the intent to conceal a criminal record, or to falsify his age, is guilty of a crime and is subject to court martial and may be sentenced for a period of five years in Leavenworth or whatever a court martial may direct.

Jeff was reeling after the lieutenant finished. Although he had heard this passage before, it had never affected him this way. This article spoke directly to him. He was a criminal and it made him sick. All night, he lay awake in his bunk trying to determine what course of action he should take.

This was not a matter he could ignore. He had to confront his problem and he had to do it quickly. Somewhere in his reverie, between sleep and consciousness, he remembered a passage Mama

Essie had read to him from the Bible. "You shall know the truth and the truth shall set you free." Well, tomorrow, he would tell the truth and he hoped that it would set him free. He also hoped that he could remain a soldier.

After reveille the next morning, Jeff approached First Sergeant Thomas and asked to speak with him about an urgent matter.

"Let it wait, soldier. I'm a busy man, let it wait."

"This matter cannot wait, Sergeant. It's extremely urgent."

"All right, it had better be," he said.

They stepped into the office of the first sergeant and Jeff told his whole story, from beginning to end. The first sergeant looked at Jeff. Contempt was written all over his face.

"This is the biggest bunch of bullshit I've ever heard. Get the hell out of here and do your job!"

"But, Sergeant . . . ," Jeff protested.

"Get the fuck out of here," the sergeant shouted.

"Okay, Sergeant. I'm leaving. But I want the record to show that I did, voluntarily, tell you my true age and that I lied to get into the Army."

Jeff turned to leave and Sergeant Thomas said, "Don't you walk out of here. Sit your black ass down, right here, until I get the captain!"

Captain O'Hara was a very imposing character—six feet, three inches tall and every inch the Academy graduate.

"So, you enlisted in the Army before your eighteenth birthday, did you?"

"Yes, sir, I did."

"And your parents have no knowledge of your whereabouts?"

"That's correct, sir."

"You are a scheming coward! You're a goldbrick. In time of war, your kind always comes forward. You're a coward. You're afraid to face the enemy. If I had my way, I'd put a bullet through your brain, right now!"

All of this, coming from the officer who, just a few short months ago, had told him that he had a future in the Army. All of the emotion that had been pent up inside him for the last eighteen months suddenly came to the surface. Jeff's anger was running wild. He could no longer control his anger or his tongue.

"Captain . . . ," he said.

"Shut up!" the captain replied. "I could have you thrown into the guard house this minute, and I may do just that!"

Jeff was on his feet now. He could sit no longer. The chair seemed to squeeze his body so he was compelled to stand.

"Captain, sir," Jeff shouted, "you do whatever you have to do! I don't give a damn what you do! I did what I had to do, even though it took me a long time to do it. I came in here and I told you the truth. You don't know anything about the forces that brought me here, and you called me a 'coward.' When I was just a child, my father was almost hanged by the Ku Klux Klan. I witnessed this through the eyes of a six-year-old boy. My whole family witnessed it."

The captain raised his hand for Jeff to shut up.

"No, sir, I will not be quiet until I have my say. If I go to Europe or the Pacific, at least I'll know who the enemy is. He won't be wearing a hood or a white robe. My weapon will be equal to his weapon. The Klan didn't give us this option. Now, sir, if you think that I'm a coward, if you think I'm trying to avoid overseas service, take your forty-five-caliber pistol from your holster and put a bullet through my brain. If you can't do that, then I say you're a fucking coward. Go ahead, sir. Do your fucking duty. Shoot!"

Captain O'Hara instructed First Sergeant Rogers to call the provost marshall and give him a rundown on what had just taken place. He further asked that the provost marshall send two military policemen to arrest Jeff.

After much consultation between the two sides, the provost marshall himself came to the company with two military policemen. He recognized that the Army had an explosive problem on its hands and that arresting Jeff for telling the truth was not the solution.

The provost notified the post commander of the incident. The post commander directed that Jeff be brought to his office. When all parties had arrived at the post commander's office, they were ushered into the conference room. For two hours, the post commander and the Judge Advocate General interrogated Jeff. The JAG allowed Jeff to tell his story from the beginning.

"Leave nothing out, soldier," the JAG instructed.

Jeff left nothing out. He told of Sergeant Faulkner's recruitment and how he falsified his age and his parents' signatures.

"Did you know that the time may come when you would have to do combat for this country?" the JAG asked.

"Yes, sir."

"Would you volunteer to go into combat?"

"No, sir, but if ordered, I would go without hesitation."

"Do you wish to get out of the Army?"

"No, sir."

"Then why are you here, soldier?"

"Sir, I needed to set the record straight and stop living this lie."

"Do you feel better now that you believe that you set the record straight?"

"Yes, sir."

"How do you feel, soldier?"

"Free, sir. I feel free."

"If what you've told us is true, then I would say you are not a coward, but a very brave young man."

"It's true, sir. Every word is true."

"Now, soldier, we come to the big test—the test of verifying what you've told us. Give me your parents' phone number."

At this, a broad smile crossed Jeff's face.

"Let us in on the joke, soldier. What's so funny? Let us in on your private joke."

"Sir, I don't mean to be funny. And I certainly mean no disrespect. But you asked for a phone number. My parents can hardly put enough food on the table. We have no phone."

"Is there someone near your parents that we could call to get in touch with your family?"

Jeff thought for a few moments.

"Yes, sir, there is. There's a grocery store a block or two from my parents' home. They could get in touch with my mother."

"What's the name of the store? What street is it on?"

"The name is 'Shaggert's Grocery Store' and it's on East Newton Street."

The JAG instructed the office clerk to try to get someone at Shaggert's Grocery Store on the phone. Meanwhile, the JAG returned his attention to Jeff. It seemed obvious to Jeff that the JAG was not out to get him. He was simply on a truth-finding mission. This full colonel asked probing questions, but he did so in a non-threatening manner.

"How long had you been planning to falsely enlist in the Army, Sergeant?"

"Sir, I didn't plan to enlist in the Army. It was a spur-of-the-moment thing. The recruiting officer approached me."

"Did the recruiting officer urge you to misrepresent your age?"

"No, sir."

"Did he ask you to forge you parents' signatures?"

"No, sir."

"Do you think he had a reason to believe that you had done anything wrong?"

"Sir, the recruiting sergeant had no reason to believe any such thing."

"Who do you think is at fault here, Sergeant? You have absolved the recruiting officer. Who do you think is at fault?"

"I am, sir. No one should be held responsible in this whole matter except me."

"Do you believe that you were insubordinate when Captain O'Hara, your company commander, spoke to you?"

"Yes, sir, I was insubordinate, and for that I apologize."

"Why were you insubordinate?"

"Well, sir, Captain O'Hara accused me of being a coward. He said I was afraid to face the enemy. He said I was a goldbrick trying to run away from the Army. I was only trying to put a stop to the big lie I had told to enlist in the Army. I was looking for a way to

reunite with my family. I was not, sir, trying to run from the Army.
I was trying to run to the Army."

The office clerk reentered the conference room and stood rigidly
at attention. The JAG appeared not to notice. His ocean blue eyes
stared into Jeff's eyes. Neither appeared to blink.

"Sir," the clerk said, "I have Mr. Shaggert on the phone."

The colonel diverted his eyes from Jeff and said, "Thank you."
He picked up the phone sitting in front of him.

"Hello. Am I speaking to Mr. Shaggert?"

"Yeah. This is John Shaggert."

"My name is Colonel Haviland and I'm calling from Fort
Wadsworth on Staten Island, New York. I have, sitting before me
here, a soldier. His name is Jeff Wiggins. This soldier is telling us
that he ran away from home about two years ago and joined the
Army. Do you know a Wiggins family?"

"Yes, sir, I know them."

"Do they have a son named 'Jeff'?"

"I don't know, sir. They have a whole bunch of chillun. I do
know that a boy of theirs is missing."

"Is that boy's name 'Jeff'?"

"I never know'd all their names, but the one that's missing is
called 'Woodly'."

"Mr. Shaggert, just hold for a minute if you can."

"I can hold on. I got nothin' else to do. Business is bad. People
just don't have money to buy stuff like they used to."

"Thank you, Mr. Shaggert."

Colonel Haviland turned to Jeff. He hesitated for a few
seconds and then asked, "Do you have a middle name or a
nickname?"

"Sir, I have no middle name, but I do have a nickname."

The colonel sounded a bit irritated. For the first time in their
long conversation, his tone had changed.

"All right, Sergeant. What is your nickname?"

"It's 'Woodly', sir."

The colonel exhaled and returned to the phone. "Thank you,
Mr. Shaggert. I appreciate you talking to me."

"Is he the one?" Mr. Shaggert asked.

"He appears to be the one," the colonel replied.

Colonel Haviland returned his attention to Jeff. "Sergeant," he said, "without getting into the legal ramifications of this whole matter, I want to say to you that I appreciate you coming to us and telling the truth. Now, we have to get in touch with your parents. We'll try to do this through the American Red Cross. Meanwhile, you're restricted to your quarters until we hear from your parents. Do you understand?"

"I do, sir."

"Over the next few days, we'll probably be giving you a series of psychological tests."

"Do you think I'm crazy, sir?" Jeff asked.

"Far from it, Sergeant. We just need to know what makes you tick."

"Sir," Jeff said, "I understand the need for me to be restricted to quarters, but I do have a request."

"What's your request?"

"Over the past several months, I've been going to the public library here on Staten Island. I've been studying with Mrs. Merrill, one of the librarians."

"What are you studying?" the colonel asked.

"Just things I feel I need to know."

"What are those things?"

"English, literature, philosophy, and ethics, sir."

Colonel Haviland thought for a minute and then replied, "The more I talk to you, Sergeant, the more I learn about you. I'll arrange for you to be driven to the library by a senior noncommissioned officer. You may study for a period of two hours and then you must return to the post. Is that clear?" the Colonel asked.

"Clear, sir."

CHAPTER NINE

Mrs. Merrill approached Jeff on this day with the same professionalism as she had in the past. When she greeted him, she immediately sensed that something was not right.

"If there's something I need to know, I'm willing to listen," she said.

Jeff sat down in her little office and told her the whole story—how he had lied to enlist in the Army and everything that had taken place since then. Mrs. Merrill listened intently.

"How can I help you?"

"They're going to give me a bunch of tests," Jeff said. "What does all of this mean?"

Her answer was almost identical to what Colonel Haviland had told him. "They probably want to see what makes you tick—how you think, whether you are adaptable to changing situations. I just hope that the battery of tests includes an IQ test. If it does, I think a lot of people may be shocked at the results. Maybe even you, Sergeant."

Jeff continued to go to the library over the next four days. On the fifth day, Colonel Haviland ordered Jeff and his company commander to report to him in the conference room.

The jeep ride from the company orderly room to the JAG's office was the first time that Jeff had seen Captain O'Hara since the confrontation. Captain O'Hara was cool and very military, although he did say, "Sergeant, I wish you the very best for whatever that's worth. I want you to know that I mean it sincerely."

"Thank you, sir. May I speak freely, sir?" Jeff asked.

"You may, Sergeant."

"Sir, I want to apologize for the way I spoke to you the other day. I just lost my temper. I shouldn't have done that. I should have been in control of myself. Sir, you were the first man to tell me I had a future in the Army and you were also the first to call me a coward."

Captain O'Hara spoke as he looked off into the distance, "Sergeant, calling you a 'coward' was the military in me. What I'm about to say to you now represents the real God-fearing man in me. I know you're not a coward. You're a survivor and you'll survive this investigation and go on to a better tomorrow—maybe not in the Army, but in some place. Now let's get the hell out of this vehicle and get this goddamned hearing over."

The captain and Jeff walked into the conference room, appeared before the colonel and saluted.

"Captain O'Hara reporting."

"Sergeant Wiggins reporting."

"At ease," the colonel commanded.

The colonel spoke, "Sergeant, I want you to step outside. I'll call you in about ten minutes. When you come back in, there will be other officers present—the post commander, the post chaplain, and Major Avery, a psychologist."

While he was waiting to be recalled, Jeff's thoughts started to wander again. What had been the reaction of his family when they were contacted? He especially wondered about his mother's reaction. Jeff knew that he was about to be forced out of the Army. What would he do once he was back in Alabama? He had more than seven hundred dollars saved and this month's pay coming. He would turn his money over to his mother, and then he would have to find a job of some kind. But what? Delivery boy? Odd jobs? What else was there for him to do?

Captain O'Hara appeared at the door to the conference room.

"Please come in, Sergeant."

Jeff was very nervous as he entered the room. A vacant chair sat facing the board of officers who were seated around the long table.

"Be seated, Sergeant," Colonel Haviland said. "I know you're nervous about what's about to happen here. I hope that we can conclude this quickly. We're going to begin with the psychologist. He gave you a series of tests and we would like to hear the results of those tests. My guess is that you would also like to know the results, is that correct?"

"Yes, sir."

"Major Avery, give us your report."

Major Avery began reciting from a stack of documents before him.

"Sir, Sergeant Wiggins is five feet ten inches tall, his weight is one hundred sixty pounds. The results of his latest physical exam show him to be in excellent health."

The post commander interrupted Major Avery. "I think we would all stipulate the matter of the physical body, Major. Let's get to the matter of the mind. What can you tell us about this solder's mind?"

"Quite a lot, sir." said Major Avery. "This soldier was tested extensively along those lines. Sergeant Wiggins is articulate, poised and extremely intelligent. His IQ is in the range of one hundred twenty-five to one hundred thirty."

The post commander again stopped Major Avery. "In your opinion, is this soldier likely to retreat under fire?"

"No, sir. However, it is unlikely that he will ever be under fire, sir. He will be leaving the Army very soon."

"Major, give us your best advice about how a soldier with Sergeant Wiggins' mindset might act in combat."

"Sir, if I were a combat officer—and I'm pleased that I am not—I would be happy to have a company of men like this soldier."

The chaplain spoke next. He seemed to be speaking only to the post commander. "General," he said, "this soldier is very spiritual. He has a firm belief in God, although I had to pull it out of him. His life has been filled with deprivation and, at times, violence. As a six-year-old boy, he came face to face with the Ku Klux Klan. They had come to hang his father. He has no memory about life before age six or seven. It seems to be his nature to put those bitter experiences behind him and to carve out a new life for himself."

The chaplain continued, "He lied about his age to get into the Army and that's wrong. But he has come before us today to correct his lie and to tell the truth. He knew that there was a chance, a very good chance, he might have to face the enemy on the front lines. After all, sir, the world is at war. I believe that this soldier has weighed the risks—within the limits of his capacity to weigh such matters—and he believes that the risks are worth taking."

The general then turned to the JAG. "What about the matter of insubordination, Colonel?"

"Sir, this soldier sees himself as anything but a coward trying to run away from the Army. I quote his own words, 'Colonel, I was not trying to run away from the Army, I was trying to run to the Army.' Except for the lie about his age, he has been and continues to be a soldier's soldier. When he was accused of being a coward, he lost control and responded in a way that was, certainly, improper. Improper though it was, how would anyone sitting here on this board have responded if faced with a similar accusation?"

He continued, "If we fail this young man in his crisis, God help us all. This soldier could have kept quiet, kept his mouth shut, and we never would have known. But he's a soldier with a conscience and he knows that no lie can live forever. So he came forth and told us the truth. Do we now condemn the lie that he told but ignore the truth? This, General, is our burden. I hope we can make a wise decision."

The general spoke to Captain O'Hara. "Captain, as this man's company commander, you know him better than the rest of us. Can you give us some new insight into how we should handle this problem? Do you still see this soldier in the same light as you did last week or the week before?"

"No, sir, General, I do not. Sergeant Wiggins has been a good soldier, an excellent soldier, from the day he reported to my unit. He has risen from private to sergeant in a relatively short period of time. On the day he confessed his true age to me, I came to the conclusion that he was trying to avoid overseas duty. I was wrong, sir, and I'm glad that I was wrong. As the general knows, I have my orders to report to the European Theater of Operations. If I had the choice of selecting one soldier and only one soldier to go with me, this would be the soldier I would want."

"Gentlemen, I've heard enough. We're going to take a break. Report back here at thirteen hundred hours."

CHAPTER TEN

During lunch, Jeff wondered if this would be his last meal in an Army mess hall. He knew that the general was close to reaching a decision and he wanted nothing more than to remain a soldier. He also knew that his chances of remaining a soldier were slim. Perhaps he had no chance at all.

At 1300, the board of officers reconvened. Jeff took his seat in front of the officers and waited for what he was sure would be the dropping of the other shoe. The general looked at Jeff and announced that his mother had arrived during the morning hours. She was getting settled in the guesthouse at the north end of the post. She would be brought to headquarters at 1330 and she would be given a few minutes to reunite with him before speaking with the general and the members of the board of officers.

Jeff knew that his mother would arrive soon, but the news that she was already on post sent his head spinning and his heart racing. It had been almost two years since he had last seen Mama Essie or any other member of his family. What would her reaction be? Would she consider him a cruel person for taking the actions he did? Or would she try to understand the forces in his life that had compelled him to do what he did? He would do his best to make her understand, but he knew that it had been very insensitive of him to force this burden upon her for such a long time.

The clerk came into the conference room and announced to the general that Mrs. Wiggins had arrived and was seated in the adjutant's office.

"Sergeant, go and meet your mother. Report back here in twenty minutes."

Jeff had no memory of walking out of the conference room and into the adjutant's office. He just knew that, somehow, he was face to face with his mother and she was crying and hugging him. He was crying and holding on to Mama Essie as if his life depended on it. Perhaps it did.

"Thank God you're safe," she said. "I've never seen you look as good as you do now. If I'd passed you on the street, I wouldn't have known you."

As he attempted to explain his actions to Mama Essie, she stated in a firm, but low voice, that there was no need to talk about it now. "We'll have our time to go over this whole thing some other time. I came to take you back home. That's all that matters now."

"Mama," Jeff said, "I think I can understand how you've suffered because of the way I left home. But if you look at it another way, what would I be doing if I hadn't left? And what will I do if I go back? Since I left home, I've had opportunities to see and do things that I never dreamed possible. For the first time in my life, I had the chance to go to the library. The librarian taught me things that opened my eyes to a whole new world of knowledge. I've begun to believe in myself as a person—a human being. No one, not one person in the two years that I've been away from home and in the Army has called me a 'nigger'. No one has referred to me in a derogatory way. Mama, in the Army I am somebody. At home, I was a nobody. Is that what you want me to go back to?"

Mama Essie looked away from Jeff. He knew why she refused to look him in his eyes. She was crying because she was torn between what her heart was telling her was true and what her mind was telling her was practical. Her heart said to her, "This may be the best thing that will ever happen to you, son." But her mind said, "He's just a boy. Take him home."

"Son," Mama Essie said, "I need you to come home with me. A month or two after you left, your father walked out on us. It's been a struggle to keep the family together. Your older brother has discovered girls. He's not as dependable about helping out at home as he once was. Your younger brother is in school and I want to keep him there. Your sisters will probably find husbands soon. So the only real help I have is you. I know you deserve better. But what else is there left for me? Some weeks I can't even get enough money together to pay the few dollars I owe for rent. Most times it's a choice of paying the rent and not eating or eating and not paying the rent. Can you understand my predicament?" she pleaded.

Jeff was having a hard time controlling his emotions. He knew that there were things he had to say to Mama Essie and he had to say them now. If he allowed his emotions to run wild now, he knew he would never say the words that needed to be spoken.

"Mama Essie," Jeff said, "I do understand. I never forgot the struggles we had before I left home. For almost two years, I've been trying to find a way to send money home to you without revealing my whereabouts. But I never found the way. In anticipation of this very day, I saved all of the money I could save. I have more than seven hundred dollars in my locker back in the barracks. I hope this will help."

"What's important now is not the money. That will help, but the real reason I'm here is to take you home where you belong."

"Don't you see, Mama?" Jeff pleaded. "This is where I belong. This is the place for me. I can do more for you, for the family, if I can remain here. I can certainly do more than I could ever do if I'm forced to go back home."

"How can you stay here, son? They won't let you stay in the Army. You forged your papers to enlist."

"Perhaps we can find a way, Mama," Jeff said. "How, I don't know."

The clerk entered the adjutant's office and said it was time. Time to go back into the conference room and sit before the board of officers. Time to come face to face with his fate.

Seated before the board of officers, Jeff could visualize all of the things he had hoped for being taken away from him. His hopes and all of his dreams were in the hands of the board. The Articles of War clearly stated that lying about his age to get into the Army was a criminal offense, an offense that subjected the offender to prison. Jeff knew that he had lied about his age. There was no doubt about that. He had voluntarily admitted that. He had also forged his parents' signatures. It was his own admission that had brought him here today.

What was he trying to do when he told the recruiting sergeant that he was eighteen and could legally enlist with his parents' permission? Was he trying to run away from some criminal offense? Was he exhibiting real patriotism, a desire to fight against the Japanese and the Germans? Or was he in search of a better life? Maybe these were some of the questions that this board would ask him to answer. Was he up to the task of explaining his motives to the board? Could he explain his motives to himself?

The JAG spoke first. "Sergeant," he said, "it seems that we have come full circle here. In a few minutes, we will hear from your mother. But before we hear from her, I would like to hear more from you. What did you hope to gain by falsely enlisting in the United States Army?"

"I don't know that I expected to gain anything," Jeff said. "I believe that I was as much giving as gaining."

"What could you give to the United States Army, Sergeant?"

"My service, sir. I can give and have given the United States Army my very best effort."

"Are you saying, Sergeant, that you have given more to the Army than you have gotten from the Army?"

"Not at all, sir. I believe that I've gotten as much as I've given."

The general interrupted the JAG and asked a question. His manner was gentle and his voice was soothing. He was known as a tough but fair officer.

"Sergeant, can you tell us what the United States Army has given you? Take your time. It's important to me that I get an answer to my question. Take a moment to collect your thoughts if you need to."

"Sir", Jeff began, "my thoughts are very clear about what the Army has given me. There are about five words, maybe more, that I can recite as examples of what's been given to me by the United States Army. Among the more compelling words are 'dignity, respect, self-worth, opportunity, and incentive'."

"Nice words, Sergeant," the general said, "but unless you can tell me clearly what they mean to you, they remain just words. Can you explain them to me?"

"I think I can, sir," Jeff said. "General, before I ran away from home, I never knew that there was any such thing as respect for a 'colored' person. I was always a 'boy' and, many times, a 'nigger'. Having been called this so often, I started to believe that's all I was. There was no opportunity for me to prove otherwise. Where, sir, was the incentive for me to be anything except what they said I was?"

The general's features changed visibly. His face became ashen and Jeff thought he could detect moisture on his face. The general did not blink. His icy blue eyes were fixed on Jeff.

"Continue, Sergeant," he said.

Jeff started to believe that the general saw him as no other white man had ever seen him. He continued.

"Sir, since coming into the Army, I have a name and that name is backed up by a serial number—just like every other soldier. I have been judged on the basis of my performance. I have been treated with dignity and respect. And one last thing, sir—all of this has given me the incentive to do even better. It has motivated me to be a better soldier tomorrow than I am today.

"Okay, Sergeant," the general said. "I hear you loud and clear. But would you admit that when you enlisted you were a boy and that you are still a boy? Would you concede that point?"

"No, sir. I would not concede that point. The truth of this whole matter is that I was never a boy. My childhood was stolen by my environment."

"Tell us about that, Sergeant," the general said.

"Well, sir," Jeff began, "in the small shack where we lived were eleven people—my mother and my father, seven children, my grandmother and my aunt. We worked hard picking cotton. My father was a sharecropper and, unlike in previous years, we were having a banner year. We had seven to ten bales of cotton sitting in the warehouse, but we hadn't eaten in three or four days. My daddy went to the landowner and asked for permission to sell a bale of cotton so he could buy food for his family. The white landowner said, 'No, not now, the market is very erratic. Wait a day or two longer.' We waited, but permission never came. My daddy made the only decision left to him. He sold a bale of cotton and bought food for his starving family. After the sale, Daddy took half the money from the sale and left it with the owner's son.

"Late that night, we heard a lot of commotion in the yard around our shack. My brothers and sisters and I ran and opened the wooden shutters that covered our windows. In the center of our yard, a huge cross was burning. A dozen or more men wearing robes and hoods surrounded the cross. They carried rifles, shotguns and a rope. The Ku Klux Klan had come to hang my father. Daddy had done the unthinkable; he had denied the wishes of a white man in order to save his starving family. The leader of the Klansmen came to the door and my grandma met him there. She stalled him by saying the things she knew he wanted to hear.

"While all of this was taking place, my father got out of the shack, through a window. He escaped into the woods.

"General, although I was only six years old, I lost my childhood that night. The picture of the Klan and my grandma stalling them to save my father's life is seared into my brain."

The members of the board sat in stony silence for a minute or two. Each member seemed to be waiting for the general to speak. Finally, the chaplain started to speak, but he abruptly stopped in mid-sentence. His emotions were getting the better of him. A soldier was not supposed to cry.

At long last, the JAG spoke up and asked, "Why would you be so anxious to serve a country that permitted this kind of violence against you and your family, Sergeant? Why, Sergeant?"

"Sir," Jeff answered, "this is the only country I have. I have little or no knowledge about Japan, Italy or Germany. I don't know any other country. Maybe after we beat the Japanese and the Germans we can begin to build a better country here at home."

"Do you really believe that, Sergeant?" the Chaplain asked.

"I believe that, sir, and I also believe in heaven. But I recognize that it will take a lot of work to get to both places. It will take a lot of work, but I believe that we can achieve human equality in this lifetime. Otherwise, we may as well lay down our arms and congratulate Hitler and Tojo."

Jeff was asked to leave the room and Mama Essie was ushered in. She was extremely nervous before this group of officers. The JAG began the questioning.

"Mrs. Wiggins," he asked, "you are aware that your son entered the Army illegally, aren't you?"

"Yes, sir, I am."

"Had he brought papers to you to sign, would you have signed them?"

"No, sir, I would not have signed them."

"Did you have reason to believe that he might run away from home?"

"No, sir, not the slightest reason."

"Was he a troubled child? I mean, did you have problems with him?"

"No, sir. He was the one child I could always count on to help hold the family together. Jeff worked very hard and brought home the money he made. He never had much of a chance to go to school, but he always insisted that someone teach him to read better. I taught him all that I could but that wasn't enough. Jeff cleaned the yard of a retired teacher in exchange for instructions in reading and for English lessons. I wish I could have done more for him. If I could have done more, he would probably be somebody today."

"Mrs. Wiggins, what would you like us to do?" the JAG asked.

"I'd like you to let me take my boy home with me, sir."

"Mrs. Wiggins," the general spoke up, "you keep referring to this soldier as your 'boy', but he has told us that he never had the opportunity to be a child. He said he became a man at age six, the night that the Ku Klux Klan came to hang his father. Do you disagree with his statement?"

"I don't see how I can disagree, sir. That night had an unsettling effect on all of us. I think it affected Jeff most deeply."

"I think, Mrs. Wiggins, that you must come to the conclusion that you no longer have a boy. He may or may not have been a boy

that January when he ran away from home, but today he's a man
and he is somebody. Suppose he doesn't want to go home, what
then?"

"He's still my son. I'm still his mother."

"Indeed, Mrs. Wiggins, you are his mother and the final
decision about this soldier's fate must rest with you," the general
said. "I would ask that you take into consideration his feelings in
this matter. The boy who ran away from home two years ago is not
the same as you remember him. What was a boy is now a man, in
body and in spirit."

The general continued, "Age is not always the final factor in
the making of a man. Your son has proven this to all of us."

The clerk called to Jeff. "Sergeant, the board would like you
back in the conference room."

CHAPTER ELEVEN

During the half hour he had been out of the room, Jeff's mind had wandered all over the place. He was almost certain that this would be his last day in the Army. He knew that his mother was excited that she almost had him in her custody again and he didn't believe that she could be persuaded to let him go. He blamed himself for the position he was in because it was he, and he alone, who had lied.

Did he lie for a good cause? Was there any such thing as a justifiable lie? These questions arose in Jeff's mind, questions to which he had no answers.

Jeff entered the conference room again. The board directed him to be seated next to his mother. The eyes of the entire board were fixed on him. For what seemed like an eternity, no words were spoken.

Jeff scanned the faces of the officers, trying to get a reading of what they were thinking. It was impossible for him to discern anything. What Jeff saw was a group of faces focused on him. He was dead set in his opposition to returning to Alabama. He loved his family dearly, especially his mother, but he knew that if he was forced to go back home, he would not be able to provide for his family in the same manner as he could if he remained in the Army. There was still that lie he had told. How could he justify that?

"You shall know the truth and the truth will set you free," the Bible stated. Well, Jeff had finally come forward and told the truth. The board of officers had confirmed his truth through Mama Essie. Would the truth "set him free"?

The JAG spoke first.

"Sergeant," he said, "your mother is going to take you back home with her. As you clearly know, it is against the law for you to

be in the Army under the circumstances by which you enlisted.
You forged the signatures of both your parents and you lied about
your age. To your credit, you came forward to set the record straight.
This, I believe, shows how innately honest you are. Your service
over the almost two years you have been in the Army has been
outstanding. You seem to be a natural leader. Today, we do not
question your basic honesty or your leadership ability. But there
still remains the reason that brought you before us. You enlisted
in the United States Army under false pretenses. Therefore, you
must pay a penalty for your actions."

During the time the JAG spoke, the general's eyes were focused
directly on Jeff. Jeff noticed the general looking at him and it made
him very nervous. He had never so much as met a general. Now,
he was sitting in the same room, less than twenty feet away from a
two-star general. And that general was sitting in judgment of him.

The general spoke. "I have sat here—we have all sat here—all
of these hours, wasting precious time over a matter that is not too
complicated to understand. This soldier wanted to serve his country
and he found a way to do it. I don't, for a minute, condone the
way he got here. But I do admire his spunk and his guts."

"Adolf Hitler," the general continued, "is running wild all over
Europe. The Japanese hordes are slaughtering many of our gallant
forces in the Pacific. Gentlemen, we are in a fight for our way of
life. Yet we sit here pondering the fate of this soldier, who is not
just ready but, if I read him correctly, is anxious to do whatever it
takes to help this country save itself. During my almost thirty
years of service, I have seen men enlist in the Army to escape criminal
offenses, to escape jail. But this is the first time I have seen this
kind of raw courage, particularly during a war. I'm going to recess
this board for a period of one hour to give us time to reflect upon
whatever it is we are about to do. I would like the JAG to remain
for a few minutes. We are in recess for one hour."

Jeff was astonished at the turn of events. It seemed that the
general was clearly on his side. How could he profit if, indeed, the
tide was beginning to turn in a direction that was favorable to
him? Could he convince Mama Essie that the general seemed

willing to help him? He wished that she would see that this opportunity, if real, would be the best thing for him. Would she be able or willing to understand what he felt, to understand what was truly in his heart? He hoped that she would.

Away from the conference room, sitting in the mess hall over a cup of coffee, Jeff poured out his heart to Mama Essie. He told her how sorry he was for the pain and anguish he had caused her and the rest of the family. But he was convinced that he could do more for the family and for himself if the general and the board found a way for him to remain a soldier. Jeff knew that Mama Essie was desperately trying to see his side of things, but he also knew that she was frightened by what the general had said about the war in Europe and the Pacific.

"I want what's best for you," Mama Essie said to Jeff, "but you are much too young to go to war. I don't want you to come home dead and in a pine box."

"Mama Essie," Jeff replied, "I've been dead since I was six or seven years old. I kept breathing so no one bothered to bury me. When I ran away from home and enlisted in the Army, a surge of life returned. The longer I remained here, the more alive I felt. Mama, you don't want me to go to some foreign land to die and I understand that. I have no desire to die in any place, but I especially do not want to return to Alabama and die a second time."

"What makes you think the general is thinking about helping you stay in the Army?" Mama Essie asked. "I don't know what to do or say. I hope the Lord will give me the answer before we go back into that room."

The minutes were ticking away and it was almost time to return to the conference room. Jeff's mind was spinning almost out of control. What would he say if the board asked him to say something more to support his reason for lying to get into the Army? He was deep in thought when the clerk came into the mess hall and said it was time to return to the conference room.

Jeff took a good look at his surroundings. He took in the military order of things, the smell of food being prepared in large quantities. Sadly, he was aware that this could be the last time he would see

these sights and smell all of these smells. Could he survive back in
Alabama after seeing and doing all that he had done over the past
two years? Jeff doubted that he could.

Seated in the large conference room, facing these military
officers, Jeff was trying to prepare himself mentally for the decision
he feared was about to come. Mama Essie was seated next to him.
The general spoke again.

"Sergeant," he said, "in ordinary times, we probably would
have kicked you out of the Army for the offense you committed.
But these are not ordinary times. This country is at war. The world
is at war. And, from all of the information available to me, you are
no ordinary soldier. Although you deceived a lot of military people,
I don't believe that you intended to conceal anything except your
age. I believe that you concealed your true age for the purposing of
serving your country—a country, I might add, that has not always
served your best interests. Now, before I tell you of our plans for
you, I have a few more questions that I would like answered. First,
do you agree with the statement that I just made?"

"Yes, sir, I agree fully."

"If we could put all this behind you, what would be your
fondest wish, Sergeant?"

"To remain in the United States Army, sir."

"It's likely that if you remain in the Army you'll have to serve
in some foreign country, maybe in a combat operation. Does that
bother you?"

"No more or less than it bothered the thousands of men who
have already been put in that situation, sir."

"Will you go overseas willingly?"

"Sir, to me, it's not a matter of going willingly. It's a matter of
doing the duty assigned. If I remain in the Army and I'm called
upon to go overseas or any place else I'll do my duty to the very
best of my ability. Does that answer your question, sir?"

For the first time, Jeff thought he saw a faint but fleeting smile
cross the general's face.

"Yes, Sergeant," the general said. "You have answered my
question more fully than you realize. I have no further questions

for now. But I reserve the right to ask a few questions or to make a few comments later."

The JAG looked at Jeff and said, "Sergeant, I have just a few more questions and I hope we can wrap this process up before too much more time has elapsed. If you are forced out of the Army and returned to Alabama, what will you do with your life?"

"That's a tough question, sir. I suppose I could go back there, suppress all of my emotions and just die again. But I'm not inclined to do that. Maybe I'll be forced to find a place to go where I can live as a person."

"Are you saying, Sergeant, that there's a high probability that you'll run away from home again?"

"Yes, sir, I'm saying exactly that."

"Why would you consider running away after what you have been through here?" the JAG asked.

"Sir," Jeff said, "I don't want to take a lot of the board's time on my personal issues, so if I decline to go into my reasons for running away a second time, I hope you'll understand."

"Make us understand, soldier," the JAG said, his voice rising. "Don't you understand that a life is at stake—your life? Now start any place you'd like, take whatever time you need, but make us understand."

"I'll try, sir," Jeff began. "Sir, for the years I lived at home before enlisting in the Army, I lived a life of constant strife and turmoil. My parents did their best to take care of us properly. But they, too, were victims of their surroundings. I was only able to go to school about a third of the time. The rest of the time was spent working at various stores as a delivery boy or doing odd jobs to help my family to keep a roof over our heads and to eat.

"At work, I was called all kinds of names and pushed around. I was generally treated as a non-person. I saw horses and other animals treated far better than I was often treated. So, the day I went to the post office to make a delivery, the day that Sergeant Faulkner said I could join the Army if I was eighteen, was the day I saw my only opportunity to escape from the miserable life that I was living. I reasoned that, if I was in the Army, I'd have a chance to help my family more than I could if I remained at home.

"Sir, the opportunity was there and I seized it. It was not a premeditated move. It was just a spur-of-the-moment action. This, sir, is how I got here. This is how I got to this room. Am I willing to go back to that life? The answer is 'no, no, no, a thousand times no.' I may have to go back, but I don't have to stay."

When Jeff finished speaking, the room was silent, deafeningly silent. The board of officers stared straight ahead. Jeff had difficulty believing that he had unburdened himself of the things that had plagued him all of his conscious life. But he felt better. He was more relaxed and it seemed to him that his thinking was much clearer than it had ever been. Jeff reasoned that he had told the truth about his feelings and he did, indeed, feel free.

The chaplain spoke next. His remarks were addressed to Mama Essie. She had been sitting in stony silence while her son, Jeff, addressed the board. She had always known that his was not a life that any child should be forced to live. She did not, however, know the true depth of his feelings. She had learned more about her son over the last few minutes he had been speaking to the board than she had learned over all of the previous years.

"Mrs. Wiggins," the chaplain said, "what is your reaction?"

"I hardly know what to say or to think," Mama Essie said. "No child should be forced to live the life Jeff has lived. But he has lived and he has survived. We've always done the very best we could for our children. But we always seemed to fall short. Jeff was never able to attend school as he should have. It took all we could do just to feed the family. Even then, we were often hungry. Jeff worked at a drug store, cleaning up and delivering things. He did odd jobs, cleaning yards and doing just about anything that would pay a little money. He never kept much of anything for himself. He brought home almost every penny he earned," Mama Essie said.

"What did you think had happened to your son when you realized that he was missing?" the Chaplain asked.

Tears started to run down Mama Essie's cheeks. "I didn't know what to think. I tried not to think. I lost many nights' sleep."

"You must have had some ideas about where your son had disappeared to," the chaplain pressed her for a reply.

Mama Essie exhaled, leaned forward in her seat, and spoke in a loud, slow voice. "Where we live, sir, it's not all that unusual for a 'colored' man to come up missing or to be killed. I did wonder if he had been taken by a group of white men and lynched. I'd witnessed lynchings before. God forbid, but this could easily have happened to my boy. Jeff looked older than he was and I was afraid that he may have been mistaken for a man and been killed."

"I have no other questions," the chaplain said.

The JAG announced that he had two or three more questions to ask before bringing this hearing to a close.

"Mrs. Wiggins," he began, "it appears that in a day or two you'll be back in Alabama with your son. Do you see things then as being different than they were in the past?"

"I hope so, sir, but I don't think so."

"What kind of job will your son be able to get when he's back home again?"

Before Mama Essie could reply, the general interrupted.

"I've heard some unbelievable stories coming from this soldier and, as unbelievable as they are, I believe every word that I've heard. Now we're starting to talk about when he gets back home. He's clearly stated that, if forced to go back home, he'll run away again. Sergeant," the general asked, "is this your position? Will you run away again if forced to go home?"

"I will, sir."

"Where will you go?"

"I don't know, sir, but somewhere that will allow me to live like a decent human being."

"Do you understand how much it will hurt your mother if you run away again?"

"Yes, sir, I do. But I also understand that it would hurt her to have me back home with nothing to look forward to—no future, no livelihood and, perhaps, no life."

"Now, Mrs. Wiggins, let me turn my attention to you. You've

heard the same words from your son as we've heard. Do you still insist that you'll take him back with you?"

"Yes, sir," Mama Essie replied, "I intend to take him home with me."

"He has said—and I, for one, believe him—that he intends to run away again. Do you still hold to this position, Sergeant?" the general demanded.

"I do, sir."

Jeff felt bad, making this admission in the presence of his mother. But in his heart he knew that going back home and remaining there was something he would not be able to do. The Army had given him new hope and a determination to redirect his life in a way he would never be able to do in any other place.

The general continued, "We have quite a problem here, Mrs. Wiggins. If this soldier could stay in the Army, if we could find a way—and this is a very big 'if'—not only will we be able to salvage a life worth salvaging, but also the country will retain a very fine soldier. Is this an effort worth pursuing, Mrs. Wiggins?"

Mama Essie thought for a moment and then said, "General, he belongs at home."

"That may very well be, but he will not remain there."

"Where could he go?" Mama Essie questioned.

"I don't know," said the general, "but go he will. I promise you, he will go."

The general continued to speak. "As his mother, the ultimate decision is yours. You have the authority to take him wherever you desire. But we here in the United States Army have a responsibility, too. We should have been able to see that the information on his application was false. But we failed. Now we say we are going to send him back to an environment that he fought desperately to get out of. Are we missing something?"

"What do you suggest I do, sir?" Mama Essie inquired.

"I don't know," the general said. "It's not so much what you can do, Mrs. Wiggins. I believe that the question is, what, together, can we do to save this soldier?"

Mama Essie took a deep breath and then sighed. "I'm willing

to listen, General."

The general looked at Jeff and then focused his eyes on Mama Essie.

"Mrs. Wiggins," he said, "I want you to take your boy, your son the soldier, and step into the adjutant's office next door while I meet with these officers. Give us twenty or thirty minutes and we'll bring you back here."

CHAPTER TWELVE

Sitting outside the conference room in the small anteroom provided by the adjutant, Mama Essie was ready to talk. She started with a question.

"Did you really mean it when you said you'd run away again if you have to go back home?"

"I did mean it and I still mean it. But, Mama, let me talk for just a minute, please. I didn't run away from you and my family. I love all of you more than anything in the world. I hope that you can believe that. I ran away because I could no longer see you struggle to keep us together. There never seemed to be enough food. None of us had decent clothes. Outside of our home, I was tired of being pushed around, being called a 'nigger', being afraid to express my thoughts.

"Daddy did the right thing by us. He sold that bale of cotton to buy food and look what happened to him. The Ku Klux Klan didn't lynch him that night, but only because they couldn't find him. That's not the kind of life I want for myself or for my family. I ran away because I believed I could do more for my family and for myself if I left. I didn't plan to join the Army. But the opportunity came and I took it. Maybe this is my destiny, I don't know. But I do know that I can never go back to the life that I lived before coming here."

Mama Essie was crying now and Jeff was sorry to see that. He knew that she, too, had lived a hard life, much harder than his life had been. She had endured that hardship for a much longer period of time.

She dabbed at her wet eyes and said, "Things will get better in time, son. I hope you can exercise a little patience."

"Mama, Daddy exercised patience and we almost starved to death. Things will only get better for us when we decide that we can no longer tolerate our present condition and when we start to do something for ourselves. We live in two worlds, Mama—a 'colored' world and a white world. Both worlds are controlled by white people."

"I didn't see any 'colored' officers in that room," Mama Essie said. "They were all white men. What's the difference?"

"The difference," Jeff said, "is that these men are more interested in accomplishing a mission than they are in the color of my skin. They're not perfect. But they're light-years ahead of the white men I knew back home. I have a sense of self here. I never had that in Alabama and, if I have to go back, I don't see things there being any different than they were in the past."

This time, the adjutant, a lieutenant colonel, came into the anteroom and said that the board was reconvening. As they started to leave the room, the adjutant said, "Sergeant, I wish you good luck."

"Thank you, sir," Jeff said. "I believe that I'm going to need it."

The JAG spoke first.

"Mrs. Wiggins," he said, "the general has come up with a possible solution. Nothing is certain yet. The general's on the phone now talking to the War Department. Before he comes back into the room, we need to clarify a few things with you. The general is trying to get a waiver from the secretary of the army. What this means is simply this—with your permission, we would change your son's record to reflect his true age. You would, in turn, sign an affidavit that gives permission for him to remain in the United States Army. Is this something you would be inclined to do, Mrs. Wiggins?"

Mama Essie was clearly struggling. "I don't know, sir. I want him home with the rest of our family. He's too young to go to war and, maybe, be killed."

"You raise a very powerful rebuttal, Mrs. Wiggins. But the reality is that if you take him back home, he's not going to remain there. He's stated emphatically that he'll run away again. Wouldn't you be more contented to know where he is, to be in contact with him through letters and to know that he's happy, doing what he likes to do? The alternative, it seems to me, is frightening. If he runs away from home, you'll have no idea where he is, what his life is like, whether he's alive or dead. In the Army, his commander can compel him to keep in close contact with his family. You're correct, Mrs. Wiggins, he is too young to die on the battlefield. But every soldier who died on the battlefield was too young to die. We hope, we always hope, that no one will die. But we know that some will. Those who die, die for a great cause and they die with honor. If I have learned anything at all about this soldier, your son, I believe it would be preferable to him to die with honor—if that comes to pass—rather than to die with a yoke around his neck as is possible if he returns home or runs away again. Are those your sentiments, Sergeant?" the JAG asked.

"Precisely, sir," Jeff answered in a loud, clear voice.

"May I have your answer, Mrs. Wiggins? You may make any statement you care to make before this board."

Mama Essie began quietly, "When I came here, it was with one purpose. That purpose was to take my boy and get back home as quickly as possible. Now I realize that if I had done that I would have missed a real opportunity—the opportunity to know my son better, to know what's in his heart and his soul and his mind. Today, I feel like I've been born again. I no longer see a boy who is my son. I see a man, a soldier, and a potential leader. I'm his mother. I want the best for him. I can't take this great opportunity away from him. If a life in the Army is what he wants I won't stop him."

Mama Essie turned to Jeff. She said, "Son, the Good Book says 'and a little child shall lead them'. I believe you've led us all well. Have a great journey. I pray that God will be with you all of the way."

"Amen," intoned the chaplain.

Jeff was certain that Mama Essie had touched the hearts of everyone in the room. The chaplain whispered something to the JAG and no one said a word for about two or three minutes. Finally, the JAG said, "Let's all take a ten-minute break, get a cup of coffee, and return here."

As the group was leaving the conference room, the chaplain and the JAG came over and said, "Sergeant, you go on to the enlisted men's mess and get your coffee. I don't believe you would mind if your mother had coffee with us in the officer's mess hall, would you?"

"Not at all, sir," Jeff said. "It would please me greatly."

In the mess hall, Jeff felt better than he had since enlisting in the Army. He now knew that the general was on his side. Why else would he go to the trouble of calling the War Department? In silence, Jeff prayed that the general would get an affirmative answer. He refused to speculate on what a negative response would mean for his life.

"Think positive thoughts," Jeff kept telling himself. "Think positive thoughts."

When the ten-minute break was over, Jeff arrived in the conference room and found Mama Essie and the board already there. The general was standing near the rear corner of the room, talking with Mama Essie. Jeff did not approach them. He knew that you only approached a general when you were invited or told to do so. Jeff stood next to his seat in the conference room. He would not sit until told to do so. This was just plain old good military courtesy.

Finally, the general took his seat along with the other officers and said, "Be seated, soldier."

Jeff became a little disturbed because Mama Essie was now seated alone in the back of the conference room. What did all of this mean? Was the general about to announce that he was unable to secure the permission of the War Department to correct his age and allow him to stay in the Army? Was this a signal that he was about to be kicked out of the Army and sent back to Alabama? Before Jeff could ponder the questions he had asked himself, the general began speaking.

"Sergeant," he said, "I have just gotten off the telephone with both the assistant secretary and the secretary of war. I had some difficulty securing permission to correct your age and retain you in the United States Army. However, after much discussion, my views prevailed. I was able to prevail because I sold you as one of the best soldiers in the United States Army today. I told the secretary that you have not yet reached your full potential. I believe everything I told the secretary. Now it's up to you to continue to prove me correct. Just continue to be the best soldier you can be and all of us will benefit."

The general continued, "You have a great mother, soldier. None of this could be done without her cooperation and consent. She is not happy about the possibility that you and others like you may, someday soon, find yourself in the line of fire. Neither am I happy about this. But, again, the world is at war. We'll be forced to fight in places not of our choosing. But, with a dedicated cadre of people like you, we will prevail.

"On behalf of this board, Mrs. Wiggins, thank you. I have every reason to believe that before this war is over, your son will make you proud. He will, I believe, make us all proud."

The general turned to the JAG and said, "Colonel, my work here is finished. You will see to it that all of the administrative details in this matter are properly executed and that this soldier is placed on a fast track, where his skills and dedication will be properly utilized."

"Yes, sir," the JAG replied.

When the general pushed his chair back in preparation to leave the room, the board of officers and Jeff rose and stood at rigid attention. The general's aide, a captain, stepped into the room and handed the general a large military envelope.

"What is it?" the general demanded.

"Sir, it is confirmation of your conversation with the secretary regarding the status of this soldier."

"Very good," the general said.

The general walked over to where Mama Essie was sitting and said, "Mrs. Wiggins, you have made a wise decision. As time goes by, you—along with the rest us—will be able to see just how wise and far reaching a decision this was."

He shook hands with Mama Essie and turned to Jeff.

"Sergeant," he said, "we have gone to the mat on your behalf.

Keep your life and your work in focus, remain dedicated and good things will happen to you."

"Thank you, sir," Jeff replied. "I owe it all to you. You have given me a new life."

As the general was departing, Jeff saluted with tears of joy in his eyes. He tried to tell himself that a soldier is not supposed to cry. But, because it was impossible to suppress his tears, he thought, "To hell with protocol. It's not everyday that a general gives you a new life."

CHAPTER THIRTEEN

With the general's departure, a flood of activity began in the conference room. The JAG walked over to where Mama Essie and Jeff were standing. He thanked Mama Essie for her participation and cooperation in bringing this matter to a successful conclusion. He said the necessary papers were being prepared for her signature and would be ready within an hour. Arrangements had been made for her to spend another night in the guesthouse. The post commander's staff car would take her to Grand Central Station in Manhattan the next morning. Meanwhile, the post commander said that Jeff and his mother were free to walk around the post, get reacquainted or do whatever else pleased them.

Jeff and Mama Essie walked toward the PX. It was the first time they were able to talk with this whole ordeal behind them. Seated in the PX, Jeff saw Corporal Mitchell. He gave Mitchell the key to his footlocker. He instructed him to look in the very bottom of the locker and to bring the large envelope that was stored there back to the PX. The envelope contained a little over seven hundred dollars, the money Jeff had been saving since the day he entered the Army. This was the first time he had been able to get money to his family without fear of revealing his whereabouts. He was aware of the struggles his family had to be going through back home. This money would go a long way toward relieving a part of those struggles.

Seated in the PX, Mama Essie turned to Jeff. "Did I make the right decision or will I sign your death warrant when we go back to post headquarters?"

"Mama, you made the right decision and I thank you for it. When you sign the papers, I'd rather think of it as a resurrection proclamation. When you put your signature on those papers, I'll be alive, truly alive, for the first time. For me, life now has a meaning. I feel like a human being that has some value. It's a feeling I never had before, one that I never thought I would have."

"Just write to us, keep in touch with us. Let us know how you're doing. We worry about you all the time and we pray for you every day," Mama Essie pleaded.

"I will, Mama, I will," Jeff promised.

Corporal Mitchell returned to the PX with the large envelope containing the money Jeff had saved. Jeff handed the envelope to his mother.

"This is the money I couldn't give you until now. I know that the little money I made before I left home wasn't very much, but sometimes it made the difference between eating and not eating. Now that we have matters straightened out with the Army, things will be better for you and for me. I'll arrange for the finance officer to forward three-quarters of my pay to you. This way, no matter where I am, you'll always get the money on schedule," Jeff told Mama Essie.

"I don't know what to say," Mama Essie said.

"Don't say anything, Mama. Just use the money for the things you need. It's time for us to get back over to the JAG's office."

As they walked back toward the office, Mama Essie asked Jeff if he knew how long he would remain on this post.

"I don't know how long I'll be here," he replied. "Some units may be leaving soon. I don't know if I'll be among those going."

"Does it scare you that you might have to go?"

"Not at all, Mama. I wouldn't volunteer to go. But, if I have to go, I'm ready."

Mama Essie's face turned grim. She said nothing more about the subject.

Upon their arrival at the JAG's office, Mama Essie was given several papers to read and sign. Satisfied with what the papers contained, she signed them hurriedly. Jeff watched her and got the impression that she had to sign the papers quickly before she changed her mind.

The personnel chief took the papers and said that the JAG would like a few minutes with Jeff and his mother before Mama

Essie left. A few minutes later, the JAG stepped into the personnel chief's office, took a look at the signed documents and turned to Mama Essie.

"Mrs. Wiggins," he began, "I cannot begin to imagine the ordeal you must have gone through to wake up one morning, find your young son gone and have to wait almost two years before finding him. Allowing this soldier to remain in the Army and to serve his country is a testament to your courage and compassion. I thank you, the Army thanks you and I know that your son thanks you. At o-nine hundred tomorrow, a staff car will be at the guesthouse to drive you back to the train station for your trip home. Good luck and God bless you."

Mama Essie said nothing. She extended her hand. The JAG took it and she turned and almost raced out of the room. What Jeff knew, that the JAG did not know, was how Mama Essie appreciated the manner in which she had been treated while at Fort Wadsworth. For the first time in her life, she had been treated with the respect due her. No white person had ever addressed her as "Mrs". At home, it was almost as if she had no name or was unworthy of any kind of respect. For those white people who knew her name, she was simply "Essie"; for those who did not know her name, she was "you" or, in some cases, "aunt". She noticed the respect she had been given and Jeff could only hope that Mama Essie understood how he felt when he talked about being so disrespected that he almost began to feel like a nobody, a non-person.

Captain O'Hara came out of the personnel office to shake hands with Jeff's mother and to say "goodbye". Jeff was a little uncomfortable in front of his company commander. He kept thinking about the confrontation they had when he first revealed his true age. The captain had accused him of being a coward and he had exploded. Would the captain hold this against him?

After saying goodbye to Mama Essie, Captain O'Hara turned to Jeff.

"Welcome home, Sergeant," he said. "Nothing has changed. I still believe that you have a great future in the Army and I'm going to do my damnedest to see to it that you achieve it."

Before Jeff could reply, the captain was gone.

After having dinner in the non-commissioned officers' mess, Jeff and Mama Essie retired to the guesthouse where she was staying. They talked late into the night. Jeff's primary concern now was his father. Why had he left the family?

Mama Essie was very composed and deliberate in her explanation. "Your daddy," she said, "had been despondent for a long time. Even before you left, I could see the changes in him. He was ashamed because he couldn't provide for his family as he wanted to. He was upset that his children couldn't attend school regularly. He kept asking himself, 'What do I have to do to be considered a man?' It seemed that no matter what he did, no matter how hard he worked, in the eyes of white people, he was just an overgrown boy, at best, and a good-for-nothing nigger, at worst.

"So, one day," Mama Essie continued, "he just left."

"Where did he go?"

"I'm not sure, but we heard that he went to Milwaukee. We never heard from him, so I can't be sure where he is."

"How did you keep things together with Daddy and me gone?"

"We did the best we could. With the war going on, people had a few more dollars to spend, so my dressmaking helped us to keep our heads above water most of the time. But it hasn't been easy."

"I'm sorry, Mama. I'm sorry I haven't been able to help you until now. In that envelope is a little more than seven hundred dollars. I hope it will help. I also hope that better days are ahead for all of us."

CHAPTER FOURTEEN

At 0900 the following morning, a staff car with a military driver was parked in the front of the post guesthouse. The car was waiting to take Mama Essie to the train station. As Jeff placed her bag in the car, the driver announced that he had been instructed to await the arrival of the chaplain before proceeding to Manhattan and the train station.

The chaplain arrived a few minutes later and said that he alone would be accompanying Jeff's mother to the train station. The chaplain felt that the trip would be too emotional for both mother and son. "Besides," he said, "the ride on the Staten Island ferry will give me some much needed time to talk with your mother. She's been through quite an ordeal."

"Does this mean that you'll be going all the way to the station with her, sir?" Jeff asked.

"That's exactly what it means," the chaplain said with a smile.

"Thank you, Chaplain," Jeff said.

Saying goodbye to Mama Essie was not easy, but he got through it. As the staff car pulled away from the guesthouse, Jeff was sad to see his mother leave, but the joy of their reunion overshadowed any sadness in his heart. It felt good to have his family back.

Jeff went back to his quarters in the company barracks feeling a sense of liberation. Just a few days ago, he had been taken from these same barracks under a military police escort. He had not expected ever to call these premises "home" again. Maybe another barracks, perhaps at Leavenworth, but not these barracks. Despite this feeling of euphoria, when he sat on his bunk he found that he was very tired. Dealing with the stress of the hearings before the board of officers as well as facing the very real threat of a dishonorable discharge and possible imprisonment had drained him of more energy than he realized. Jeff fell asleep on the bunk, fully dressed.

Several hours later, he was awakened by the first sergeant, who was standing over him. Jeff rose to his feet, unsteady and disoriented. The first sergeant broke into a smile, patted Jeff on the back and said, "You're a celebrity around here. I've been in this Army for more than twenty-five years and I never got the attention that you've gotten over the past four or five days. How in the hell did you bullshit the general into coming to your defense?"

"I have no idea, Top Sergeant," Jeff said. "I suppose the general knows a good soldier when he sees one."

He smiled. "Well, congratulations," said the first sergeant. "You may be young, but you're a man in my book."

"I appreciate that, Top Sergeant," Jeff replied.

"All right, enough of this bullshit. It seems to me that the top brass has appointed me as your guardian angel—not that you need one. Here's your schedule for tomorrow. At o-eight hundred, you'll report to Captain O'Hara. At o-nine thirty, you'll report to the battalion personnel officer and, finally, at thirteen hundred hours, you'll report to the battalion adjutant. After you've done all of those things, if there's any time left, you can go the latrine and take a piss!"

Promptly at 0800, Jeff reported to Captain O'Hara.

"Sit down, Sergeant," the captain ordered. "It seems that someone has placed you on a fast track. You'll be leaving this post in about sixty days for a new assignment. I consider it my duty to give you fair warning that the general has placed his reputation on the line by taking your case all the way to Washington. Don't prove him wrong. When you leave this office, there will be an interview with the personnel officer. He'll want to reassess your service record and find out what assignment you're best suited for. The battalion adjutant will put all of the pieces together and make the assignment to your new station. Do you have questions, Sergeant?"

"Yes, sir. I have several questions," Jeff said.

"Fire away, Sergeant."

"Sir, you stated that I have about sixty more days to remain on this post. Do you know where I'll be assigned?"

"No, I don't. All of that will be up to the adjutant and the personnel officer. But your new assignment is high priority. The general's fingerprints are all over it."

"Will I continue in my same assignment during my remaining time here?"

"Yes, you will, much to my regret. Personally, I'd like to assign you to a platoon sergeant's position, but you're on hold until you reach your new station."

"Thank you, sir," Jeff said. "I have no further questions."

As Jeff rose, saluted and prepared to leave, the captain spoke again. "Tell me about your trips to the library."

Jeff related all of the things that Mrs. Merrill had taught him over the months that he had been going to the library—the books and the papers he had read and how Mrs. Merrill had taught him to be more poised and self-confident.

"Do you plan to continue seeing Mrs. Merrill over the next sixty days?" Captain O'Hara asked.

"Yes, sir, just as often as my duties will permit," Jeff replied.

"Sergeant," Captain O'Hara intoned in a low, but stern voice, "go to the library, find Mrs. Merrill and get a schedule of the times that she can see you. Bring that schedule to me and I'll arrange for the motor pool to transport you there and return you to the post when you've concluded your studies. Is that clear, soldier?"

"Very clear, sir."

"Now get the hell out of here," the captain smiled.

"I'm gone, sir."

CHAPTER FIFTEEN

The personnel office was a giant room filled with both military and civilian personnel. When he reported to the section chief, a master sergeant, Jeff could hear the low conversation of some of the enlisted personnel around him.

"See the skinny little mother fucker there? He's nothin' but a kid and already he's a sergeant."

"How'd he do that?"

"He kisses the general's ass, that's how he did it."

Master Sergeant Griffin heard the remarks and he responded, angrily.

"If I hear one more sound out of you two sorry excuses for soldiers, I'll have you on latrine duty for so long you'll smell like shit. Am I understood?"

"Loud and clear!" was the reply.

The personnel officer, a warrant officer, was very cordial. He immediately put Jeff at ease.

"Sergeant, I want to congratulate you for coming forward and setting this matter straight," he said. "Take a look at these papers and tell me if your true age is reflected here."

Jeff looked at the papers and confirmed their accuracy.

"Is the next of kin indicated the person you wish to be notified in case of an emergency?"

"Yes, sir."

"Is that person Mrs. Essie M. Wiggins?"

"Yes, sir."

"What's your relationship to Mrs. Wiggins?"

"She's my mother, sir."

"Will she be the beneficiary of your GI insurance, if it ever comes to that?"

"She will, sir."

"Do you wish to add anything to what we have covered here?"

"I would, sir. I'd like to arrange for a part of my pay to be sent directly to my mother."

"That's a function of the finance officer, but I'll arrange it for you. How much would you like deducted?"

"Seventy-five dollars a month, sir."

"Sergeant, the personnel officer said that your base pay is ninety-six dollars a month. If my math is correct, that leaves you a total of twenty-one dollars. Can you get by on that?"

"I can, sir, and I will."

"All right, consider it done," he said.

At 1300, Jeff reported to the battalion adjutant. Major Kelly was a jovial giant with curly red hair.

"Come in, Sergeant," the major directed. "Dammit, you look like you should be a high school freshman instead of a buck sergeant in the Army. How'd you manage to bullshit your way into the military? Actually, don't answer that. You have some very powerful brass on your side. I don't think I want to rock the boat. My job today is to find out what your vision for yourself is. What would you like to do in the Army and where would you like to do it?"

"My primary vision has already been fulfilled, sir. That was to come clean with the Army and myself and to be reunited with my family," Jeff said.

"And beyond that?"

"I don't really know, sir. I'm sure that I can benefit from your guidance."

"Sergeant, don't waste my time jerking me around. It says here," as he pointed to a stack of papers on his desk, "that you have an IQ of almost one hundred thirty and you're asking me to believe that you have no vision beyond the one you just stated?"

"Sir, I'm not asking you to believe anything. I'm telling you the facts as I see them! I want to be the best soldier possible. Where that ambition takes me is yet to be determined."

The major smiled. "Keep your powder dry, Sergeant. The JAG told me that if I wanted to see your true colors I'd have to put your back against the wall. I like what I see. Your colors suit me just fine. You'll receive a new assignment within the next sixty days. Would you like to remain in an administrative role or would you like to be assigned to a field position?"

"A field position, sir," Jeff answered.

The adjutant asked several more minor questions before he called the sergeant major into his office. The sergeant major had control of all enlisted men's records.

"Sergeant Major," the adjutant said, "what, if any, vacancies are there in the table of organization of the seven hundred thirty-first?"

"I'll have to look at their organization, sir," the sergeant major replied.

"Take a quick look and let me know."

Several minutes later, the sergeant announced that three vacancies existed in the 731st—positions for two corporals and one staff sergeant. The sergeant major turned to leave, but the adjutant ordered him to remain.

"I may need your help here, Sergeant Major," he said. "Get Captain O'Hara on the phone, but first let me bounce this idea off of you. What would be your reaction if I proposed to O'Hara that he select this soldier for the staff sergeant vacancy?"

The sergeant major hesitated for a few seconds and said, "Sir, this man is young but he's shown that he can lead. If the general is for him, who am I to oppose him?"

The adjutant smiled at the sergeant and said, "This is the biggest pile of horse shit I have ever heard from you. I didn't ask what the general is for or against. I asked for your personal reaction. Either you're for this soldier filling that vacancy or you're opposed to the idea! Which is it, Sergeant Major?" the adjutant pressed.

"I'm for it, sir," he replied.

"Now all we have to do is get Captain O'Hara on board."

"I'll get him on the phone, sir."

"Captain O'Hara? Major Kelly here. I've just been reviewing your table of organization and you have vacancies for two corporals and one staff sergeant. Would you consider Wiggins for this vacancy?"

"I'm all for it, Major, but he'll only be here for the next sixty days."

"Okay, Captain. When he leaves, we'll just have to find another man to fill his position. Send me the required paperwork. We'll start the ball rolling."

"You'll have it tomorrow, Major," promised Captain O'Hara, "and thank you for your interest. I have no doubt that this soldier will do well in that position."

"Sergeant," the adjutant said, "now you've heard everything. Do you have any questions?"

"No questions, sir, but I would like to say 'thank you'."

"You can best thank me by doing an outstanding job. Now get the hell out of here. You've taken enough of my time."

Jeff returned to his company just in time for the evening mess. When he entered the hall, he was met with total silence by the dozen or so noncommissioned officers present. He knew that his appearance before the board of officers was big news on this small post. He was content to ignore the silence, have his meal and return to his quarters to rest and to think about the fast-moving events of the past few days.

Two sergeants in his company came over and sat at the table with him. One of the men, a Sergeant Dixon, looked at him with contempt. Anger was in his eyes and it spread to consume his whole face. Jeff stopped eating and stared back at Dixon. He said nothing. He just continued to stare at Dixon, eyeball to eyeball.

Dixon spoke with a trembling voice that seethed with anger and disgust. "Who the hell do you think you are? You're still wet behind the ears. Maybe you fooled the Army, but you don't fool me. I'm forty-three years old and I've been in this Army for twenty-two years. It took me nineteen years to make sergeant and, in less than two years, they make you a sergeant. None of these men will have anything to do with you. I'll personally see to that."

Jeff said nothing. He took his tray and moved to another table. This move sent Sergeant Dixon into a yelling rage. "Don't you walk away from me, you fast-talking son of a bitch. I'll take you out into the company area and kick your ass and send you back to Alabama."

The commotion created by Sergeant Dixon spread quickly to other areas of the mess hall. Someone reported the incident to the orderly room and First Sergeant Thomas charged into the mess hall, demanding to know what the disturbance was about. Dixon was standing over Jeff, insisting that Jeff follow him to the company area where he could "kick his ass".

First Sergeant Thomas ordered Dixon to sit down. Dixon refused. "I'll tell you one last time," First Sergeant Thomas said, "then I'll knock you on your ass." Dixon got the message.

"What's going on here?" the first sergeant asked Jeff. "Tell me something quickly."

Jeff calmly related all that had happened.

"Did you say something to provoke Dixon?" First Sergeant Thomas inquired.

"I did not," Jeff said. "I had no conversation with anyone here. I'm tired and I need some rest."

The mess sergeant came over and spoke on Jeff's behalf. He told Thomas how Dixon had confronted Jeff and how he would not let up, despite Jeff's efforts to move away.

First Sergeant Thomas ordered Dixon to finish his meal and leave the mess hall. Dixon, still seething, sighed, "I'll leave. But this isn't over yet and it won't be over until I kick this son of a bitch's ass."

"Be careful, Dixon," the first sergeant said. "Your stripes are already hanging by a thread. Don't force me to break that thread. I will, if you continue this nonsense."

After reveille, First Sergeant Thomas ordered Jeff and Dixon into his office. "I'm concerned that this incident will continue to escalate, so I've reported it to Captain O'Hara. He'll see both of you at o-eight thirty. In the meantime, you will both conduct yourselves as soldiers in the mess hall. Do you read me?"

"Loud and clear," replied Jeff. Dixon, still sullen, said nothing.

As Jeff entered the mess hall, the mess sergeant met him at the door to the noncommissioned officers' section. "Enjoy your breakfast," he said. "If Dixon starts trouble again, I'm here to intervene."

"Thank you, Sergeant," Jeff said. "There will be no trouble on my part."

The mess sergeant followed Jeff as he took a seat at an empty table.

"Sergeant," he offered, "Dixon's mad at you because you accomplished in less than two years what took him almost a quarter century to achieve. He's a career soldier. He believes that it takes years to become seasoned enough to even think about advancing up the ladder to become a sergeant. Sergeant Dixon doesn't understand that we're living in a different society now where war and all that it involves is largely mechanized. It takes a new kind of soldier to fight today's war. He's not that kind of soldier and he probably never will be. You just have to go on about the business of doing your job and being a good soldier. There are lots of Dixons in this Army. Just try to avoid them. You'll never be able to change them. They march very smartly in place, but they never go anywhere. Keep your focus. It's up to you how far you go."

At 0800, First Sergeant Thomas ushered Jeff and Sergeant Dixon into Captain O'Hara's office. "Sit down, men," the captain said. Jeff recognized the tingle of irritation in his voice. "What the hell is going on here between the two of you?"

Jeff sat quietly, allowing Dixon to speak first. "Well, sir," Dixon began, "Wiggins has a chip on his shoulder. He acts as if he's better, smarter and just generally superior to the rest of us. And I don't like that. I've been in the Army for more than twenty-two years. I came through the ranks the hard way. It took me seven years to move up to private first class. This boy comes into a man's Army—arrogant, disrespectful to those who built the Army and, it seems to me, sir, that the officers are allowing him free rein. He can do no wrong. Captain, this boy is still wet behind the ears."

"Anything else, Sergeant?" the captain asked.

"No, sir," Dixon answered.

"Wiggins, what do you have to say in reply to Sergeant Dixon?"

"Not very much, sir," Jeff began. "I believe I give Sergeant Dixon the respect he's due. I don't have any social contact with him. We live in different worlds. Sergeant Dixon's idea of fun is getting drunk at the NCO club. I don't drink. Beyond this, I have nothing against the sergeant."

Captain O'Hara spoke. "Sergeant Dixon, there seems to be a bit of jealously on your part. I respect the fact that you've been in the Army for twenty-two years and that it took you almost all of those years to make sergeant. You're a career soldier and I applaud that. But you're a member of the old guard, the old Army. It seems to me that you're having difficulty recognizing that this is a new day, a new Army—one that requires bright, energetic and highly trainable young men, men who think fast and act quickly. The world is engaged in total war and this country is a leading force in the struggle. As this war progresses, you're going to meet thousands of young men like Wiggins. You'll either adapt to this new Army or it will leave you behind. When you leave this office, you will— both of you—go about your duties in a manner befitting noncommissioned officers. If, Sergeant Dixon, I hear that you have confronted Sergeant Wiggins in a hostile fashion, I will have your stripes. It that clear?"

"Clear, sir," Dixon replied.

CHAPTER SIXTEEN

Two months had passed since Mama Essie had come to the post. During this time, Jeff had gone to the library for two hours each evening to be tutored by Mrs. Merrill. Their relationship had developed into one of genuine friendship and respect. Mrs. Merrill never talked down to him; she was never condescending. But she never hesitated to express her displeasure when she believed that Jeff had not given the proper attention to his work and to the knowledge that she was trying to impart to him. Although she was a strict, no-nonsense tutor, Jeff loved this woman like a member of his family because, deep down inside, he knew that she had his interests at heart. She insisted upon his best effort.

"If you truly don't understand some of the things I tell you," she would frequently say, "it's okay. I can always find other ways to make you understand. But if you tell me you do understand and, later, I find that you didn't, that frustrates me. I consider it a waste of my time and yours. Just be honest and forthright with me and we'll both profit from that honesty."

Often, when the quiet of the night gave him time to reflect, Jeff thought of Mrs. Merrill. He could not, even in his wildest dreams, imagine being able to relate to a woman like her. What, in some ways, seemed like a few short years before, the Klan had come to hang his father in Alabama. Now, this middle-aged white woman, this librarian, was trying to open his eyes to the mystery of a world he could not have imagined a few years ago. Maybe she was an angel sent by God to administer some knowledge and kindness to a struggling young soldier. Whoever or whatever she was, she had changed his life in ways only he could understand.

About a year and a half after beginning his tutoring sessions with Mrs. Merrill, Jeff was promoted to staff sergeant and given orders to report to Fort Leonard Wood, Missouri. He would be leaving in fifteen days. He was happy about the promotion, but he was sorry that he had to leave his sessions with Mrs. Merrill. When he announced that he had his orders to leave, she smiled. "We both knew this day would come soon. If I've given you anything that you can take with you, I hope that it's knowledge of this simple fact—you are a very decent human being, gifted with an insatiable will to learn. All that I've tried to do here is to help you see yourself as a valuable person. I believe you now have a vision of where you want to go and what you'll do when you get there. Be true to yourself, my friend, and remember to write and let me know how and what you are doing."

With that, she turned her face away from Jeff and said, in a voice that was almost inaudible to him, "God bless you, son. Now be on your way. Our business here is finished. Go."

Jeff was pleased that she did not look at him. He knew that she was crying. He could feel the tears running down his own cheeks. "You're truly one of God's brightest angels. Goodbye, Mrs. Merrill. I'll always remember you."

CHAPTER SEVENTEEN

On the day of Jeff's departure from Fort Wadsworth, First Sergeant Thomas instructed him to report to the battalion adjutant before leaving for the train that would take him to Missouri. The adjutant was a bit informal. He shook Jeff's hand and said, "Sergeant, a lot of reputations are at stake here—the general's, the post commander's, the JAG's and mine. If you fail to succeed, we'll all look like fools. Go out there and show the Army what you're made of. Now get the hell out of here and be the soldier we all know you can be."

Jeff came to attention, saluted and, as an afterthought, said to the adjutant, "I won't disappoint you. All of your good reputations will remain intact. This, sir, is my solemn vow to you."

On the train headed for his new duty station in Fort Leonard Wood, Missouri, Jeff had to face a mixed sense of happiness and sadness. He was happy that he no longer had to live with the big lie that brought him into the Army. Mama Essie had her family intact again. Although he was miles away from home, his family knew his whereabouts and his mother was receiving the bulk of his pay to help her support the family and herself.

The board of officers had heard his story and they were sympathetic to his plan to remain in the Army. The general had, it seems, been impressed with his sincerity and soldierly decorum and had gone out of his way to retain him in the Army. Just days ago he had been promoted to staff sergeant. Despite being the recipient of these many blessings, Jeff felt more than a tinge of sadness.

He was well aware that much of the success he was now having was due to his association with Mrs. Merrill. She had taught him lessons that would stay with him for the rest of his life. He had learned good listening skills as well as good reading and writing skills. Even more important was the self-confidence she had instilled in him.

Jeff had asked himself many times, "Why?" Why had Mrs. Merrill gone out of her way to do all of the things she had done for him? Had she seen something in a sincere but innocent young man? Was she doing for him what she would have done for her own son if she had had one? Perhaps he would never know the answers to any of these questions. He simply accepted the fact that Mrs. Merrill had done what she had done and that he was a much better person for it. What troubled Jeff most was the feeling that he had not properly thanked Mrs. Merrill.

How could he have been more explicit in expressing his thanks and appreciation? When they said goodbye, the emotions inside him were running wild. He had tried to do all of the things she had taught him. He looked her directly in the eyes, chose his words carefully and tried to be forceful but humble. He tried to do all of these things, but tears overwhelmed him. When she said, "Go", he seized the opportunity and left the room. She must have known how grateful he was. She had to know. God, let her know.

The motion of the train, the clack of the wheels, and the fact that he was completely relaxed for the first time in weeks helped Jeff drift into a state of reverie. He did not wish to go to sleep because he had too much to think about. But sleep overwhelmed him and he had no strength left to fight it off.

CHAPTER EIGHTEEN

"Daddy, why did you do it? How could you walk away and leave your family almost destitute?"

"Don't you question me, boy! You don't have that right. What I did was my business and I don't have to answer to you. Now drop it."

Jeff could feel the anger beginning to boil inside him. This was his daddy and he deserved some measure of respect. But was it respectful to walk away from your family in the time of their greatest need?

"I think you owe us an explanation. We're your family and that should count for something," Jeff said.

"I told you to drop it, now don't mention it again! Who are you to question me? I'm your father. I don't answer to you."

Jeff's anger was boiling over now. He could no longer contain his anger or his actions.

"To hell with not being accountable. You are accountable to your family! I want some answers and I want them now!"

"Don't you cause me to lose my temper, boy," his daddy replied.

Jeff leapt to his feet in a rage.

"Daddy, I don't care! Lose your temper if you want, but give me an answer. Why did you walk away and desert your family? Answer me, I have to know!"

"It's none of your business. Now drop it!"

"Was it Grandma Dawson's business when she stalled the Ku Klux Klan while you escaped into the woods? And whose business was it when we had to move to the next county while you hid out in the woods to escape the clutches of the Klan? It is my business—this is about our family and I'm a part of that family! Dammit, Daddy, this is my business!"

Jeff's father looked as if all the blood had been drained from his body. His face was ashen and his features had the look of a ninety-year-old man.

"Son," he said, "I wasn't a man. They wouldn't allow me to be a man. I worked hard. The whole family worked hard, and they would not allow me to be man enough to sell a bale of cotton that we had grown, picked, and stored in a warehouse. I sat on the porch for four days waiting and watching my family slowly, ever so slowly, dying from hunger. When I couldn't take it any more, I acted.

"What did it get me? It almost got me lynched by that hooded mob of 'respectable' white men calling themselves 'protectors of a decent white society'."

His father continued, "Every time I looked at your mother, your grandmother, and each of you, I felt like a coward for running away into the night and leaving all of you to face that violent bunch of hoodlums. I finally decided that, if I couldn't be a man who was able to stand up for his family, the family would be better off without me.

"I hope," Jeff's father said, "that when you grow up, you'll be able to escape the kind of life I was forced to live. You know, son, to some extent, I'm still living that life. It's not quite as bad as it used to be, but it's still bad. I know that you're not able to understand now. But one day, maybe you'll understand. Try!"

"Daddy, I can and I do understand," Jeff interrupted. "But I still wish you'd stayed with us. Not only do we need you, but you also need us. We need each other."

The train came to a stop in Pittsburgh, Pennsylvania. Jeff opened his eyes and his mind was fuzzy. He had expected to be sitting across the table from his father. A sense of disappointment engulfed him when he realized that he had just experienced the most vivid dream possible.

Had he been talking in his sleep? Jeff looked around to see if there had been indications that he had been acting out his dream. Satisfied that he had not, he tried to settle back into sleep. But the dream was too real, too vivid for sleep to engulf him again.

In the dream, Jeff had criticized his father for abandoning the family, but wasn't he guilty of the very thing for which he had chastised his father? He had sneaked away from the family in the early hours of the morning, just before the break of dawn. For almost twenty months, no one in his family knew if he was alive or dead. Was this any different than what his father had done?

Jeff tried to rationalize what he had done by telling himself that his intentions were pure. Surely his family would understand that his intention had always been to help move them into a better position financially and to contact them some day. But how could he be certain that his father's intentions were any different from his own?

Who was he to judge his father? He had never walked in his father's shoes. The KKK had never come in the middle of the night to hang him, and he had never been psychologically castrated before his family's eyes.

Grandma Dawson had often said that the biggest threat to southern white society was a strong black family. "If they can divide us, they can better control us," she said.

Even Mrs. Merrill had alluded to this. She had once said that people can, fairly easily, dominate and enslave the body, but once the mind is free—the body will soon follow. Mrs. Merrill was one of the most decent human beings he had ever met.

During his early years in Alabama, he often lived in a state of reverie. His thoughts were not so much about how things were, but his thoughts were often of how things could and should be. Just as Mrs. Merrill had said, his body was beginning to follow closely behind his mind. With each passing day, it seemed that his physical being was chasing and gaining on his spiritual being.

CHAPTER NINETEEN

The pace at Fort Leonard Wood was fast and hectic. Jeff's new company commander called him into his office during the first week of his arrival. He was told in detail what the mission of his new unit was.

"We are," said his commander, Captain Kelly, "engaged in highly specialized training in preparation for being shipped overseas. Combat soldiers can only be effective when the support troops behind them are effective.

"As a support organization, our mission," Captain Kelly continued, "is to develop a system of support that will put us on the beaches or other areas of battle just to the rear of the combat troops. We'll use that support system to ensure that a steady flow of food, water, gasoline, ammunition, or other services are at their fingertips. This means that we must expect and be prepared to come under fire.

"For this mission, we've assembled two battalions of the highest-caliber men we can find. You, Sergeant, come to us recommended by no less than a two-star general. Don't let your age get in the way of your duty. There will be comments and wisecracks about a young staff sergeant. The Army is on your side. You have the same authority as any other soldier of similar rank. I expect good things from you. Do you have any questions?"

"No questions, sir." Jeff said.

"You'll be assigned as platoon sergeant of the third platoon. First Sergeant Brooks will introduce you to your men."

At reveille the following morning, First Sergeant Brooks introduced Jeff to the men of the third platoon and announced that Jeff was their new platoon leader. There were a few grunts and moans that were quickly noted by the first sergeant.

"At ease," said Brooks. "I know what some of you dumb bastards are thinking. 'They brought this boy here to lead a bunch of men.' Well this 'boy' is a staff sergeant and that equates to a man. If anyone doubts that, step forward and I'll have this sergeant, this 'boy', put his boot up your ass! Am I clear?"

"Clear, First Sergeant," was the reply.

"Good. From this point forward, we'll concentrate our attention on his leadership, not his age. At o-seven thirty, the third platoon will meet with Staff Sergeant Wiggins in the company day room."

The platoon was assembled in the day room when First Sergeant Brooks and Jeff walked in. Again, First Sergeant Brooks introduced Jeff to the platoon and left the room.

Jeff did not make a long speech. He stated very simply what his expectations were and that he would accept nothing less than the personal best of each member of the platoon. All orders were to be promptly obeyed and attention to duty was to be exercised at all times.

"Are there any questions?" Jeff asked.

A moment of silence fell over the room and then a soldier in the rear of the room rose to his feet and asked, "What year were you born, Sergeant?"

Jeff knew that this was a question designed to test his reaction. But before he could respond, another soldier—about six feet three or four inches tall and weighing in excess of 240 pounds—stood and asked, "Sergeant Wiggins, may I answer that question?"

"You may answer, soldier," Jeff said.

"The sergeant was born the same year as your mother."

Laughter filled the room, but Jeff quickly brought it to a halt.

"Gentlemen," he began, "we're not here to discuss any of our ages. I don't give a damn if any of you were born before, during or after the Civil War. What I do give a damn about is how you perform you assigned duties. In this platoon there's no room for mediocrity. Only the best is acceptable to me. We're soldiers. We will think, act and perform like soldiers at all times. The third platoon will be the platoon that sets the standard for this battalion. Any soldier failing to live up to this standard will be shipped out.

It's my job to help you get ready for the most important assignment of your lives. I don't intend to fail.

"Squad leaders and section chiefs will be held strictly accountable for the performance of all of the men assigned to them. I'll meet with squad leaders and section chiefs at sixteen thirty each day to critique the day's activities. If there are no questions, consider yourselves dismissed," Jeff said.

Over the next eight weeks, the platoon was kept very busy training for the overseas assignment that everyone knew was coming. Where the battalion would go was uncertain but rumor had it that the European theater would be their destination. The men in the platoon were now accustomed to Jeff and he to them. They admired his leadership skills and his ability to be fair. They were especially proud that theirs had been cited as the most outstanding platoon in the battalion for six of the last eight weeks.

Jeff had often heard soldiers refer to him as "a tough but fair son of a bitch." He reasoned that if one had to be a son of a bitch, fair was better than unfair.

During the ninth week of Jeff's duty at Fort Leonard Wood, First Sergeant Brooks was stricken with some type of illness that put him in the hospital. Captain Kelly, the company commander, was faced with the responsibility of appointing an acting first sergeant pending Brooks' return.

Because of Jeff's success in molding the third platoon into the best unit in the battalion, the captain sought his advice regarding the appointment.

"Sergeant," the captain said, "we don't know when, if ever, First Sergeant Brooks will come back to this unit. My first inclination is to appoint you as acting first sergeant. What are your thoughts about that? It's the highest line position a soldier can achieve in the enlisted grades in the entire United States Army. Do you feel up to the task?"

"Sir, I feel up to the task but honestly my first thoughts are of First Sergeant Brooks. I hope that he comes back soon."

"That's out of our hands, Sergeant. I spoke to the doctors at the hospital a day or two ago and it's likely that Brooks will have to remain in the States for treatment. Before I make a final decision," the captain said, "I want to speak to the battalion commander to get his views."

"Yes, sir," Jeff said.

Five days later, Jeff was appointed acting first sergeant. Two months after being appointed acting first sergeant, Jeff was officially promoted to the grade of first sergeant.

When he entered the mess hall for the evening mess, each man in his unit—192 enlisted soldiers and six commissioned officers—stood and gave a rousing ovation of approval. On this occasion, his thoughts turned to Mrs. Merrill.

She had, at times, admonished him to be humble in achieving a victory and to likewise be gracious in defeat.

"Sometimes," she said, "a very thin line separates the two."

Jeff turned to face the men in the mess hall and spoke in a loud, strong voice. "Gentlemen, thank you. It was and is your outstanding performance that made this possible. With troops of your caliber, anyone can look good. Thank you again, and don't forget, reveille is at o-six thirty!"

Captain Kelly was a young West Point graduate. He was twenty-nine years old and he was proud of the fact that he had been the moving force in getting Jeff promoted to first sergeant before the unit shipped out for overseas duty.

"First Sergeant," the captain said, "you and I are the youngest team on this post. We've made an impact on how this battalion operates. I want us to continue to do this."

"I'm a career soldier," the captain said. "A part of my career is in your hands. The extent to which you're successful impacts me directly. You're closer to the enlisted men than I will ever be and that's the way it should be. You can feel their pulse, know their thoughts, and monitor their morale. They have great respect for you and your ability. So my message to you is simple—keep it that way and keep me informed on matters that I should know about."

Jeff knew that, in part, Captain Kelly was acknowledging that, as a noncommissioned officer, Jeff was much closer to the troops than any captain could be. However, Captain Kelly's words also acknowledged the fact that, as a white officer, at that point in history, he could never relate to the black company in the way that Jeff or any other black first sergeant could.

"Whatever decisions you make about the company will have my complete support. Just bear in mind that the best interest of the company, and each man in the company, must always be uppermost in your mind."

"Thank you, Captain," Jeff said. "This unit will continue to be the best in the battalion, and I believe that you'll continue to be proud of our performance."

The platoon sergeants and the other noncommissioned officers rallied around and gave the new first sergeant their complete support. There seemed to be a new energy injected into the ranks. The company was proud of its new first sergeant and they showed it in the way that they went about their duties. There was a saying within the enlisted ranks, "Don't mess with First Sergeant Jeff. He'll reward you for good work, but he won't hesitate to kick your ass if you step out of line." Jeff was aware of this sentiment and he was careful to see to it that each soldier was recognized for his good performance.

After his promotion to first sergeant, Jeff's thoughts turned again to the circumstances and people that had gotten him to this position and this place. He wrote a letter to his mother, the person who had been the strongest and most consistent guiding force in his life. He would have loved to call her on the phone, but Mama Essie had no telephone. Jeff had to settle for a letter, sent by special delivery.

Mama Essie would be proud of his new status and Jeff knew that the whole neighborhood would know about his promotion as soon as the letter arrived. His mother was now in good shape financially compared to the time before his enlistment. She no longer had to worry about how she would feed and clothe the rest of the family. Seventy-five percent of Jeff's pay was sent directly home and he was more than pleased to be able to help his family in this manner.

After sending the letter to his mother, Jeff went to a pay phone and placed a long distance call to Mrs. Merrill. When she picked up the receiver she said, "Hello, Jeff."

"How did you know it was me?" Jeff asked.

"I usually know. Besides, who else but you would call me long distance? Give me the good news," Mrs. Merrill said.

"How do you know it's good news?" Jeff said.

"Jefferson," she replied impatiently, "I know you a lot better than you realize. There is no way you would spend this much money to call me unless you had good news."

"I do have good news, Mrs. Merrill. I was promoted to first sergeant a few days ago."

"You have my sincere congratulations, Jeff," she said. "But this is no surprise to me. Only the fact that the promotion came this soon is a bit of a surprise. I knew it would come, but I expected it to be a little later."

"I hope that I'm up to task, Mrs. Merrill," Jeff responded.

"Now you listen to me, Jeff," she said sternly. "The people who made the decision to promote you are not dummies. They know what's good for the Army and who can best fill the spots that need filling. I'll tolerate no more of your speaking this way. You're up to the task and you know it. Now work hard and start looking forward to even better things."

"Call me again before you leave for a new station," she said. "I have a feeling that you won't be there much longer. I have some reading material I'd like you to have but I want to wait until you arrive at your new station before I send it."

As Jeff was about to say goodbye, Mrs. Merrill said, "Jeff, remember, God loves you. Good things will happen to you and for you. War is dangerous and dirty, but you must use your God-given instincts and you'll be safe. In addition to God's love, which is most important, I love you, too. Don't try to reply to what I've said, just hang up and keep in touch with me."

Jeff was sure that she would not allow him to reply. His heart was so filled with gratitude that this woman had come into his life. He could not have found the proper words to reply. His eyes were blinded with tears and his vocal chords refused to utter audible sounds. Back in his quarters, Jeff stretched out on his bed. His thoughts were once again running wild.

His body shook when he recalled the words Mrs. Merrill spoke to him. What kind of person was she anyway? Certainly she was no ordinary person. All of the things she had taught him, the confidence she had instilled in him, had this all been a long, but pleasant dream? Would he soon wake up and find that the dream was now over?

In the quietness of his darkened room, Jeff could recall the time his grandmother, Grandma Dawson, had told him the story of the angel from God who had spoken to Joseph about the pregnancy of Mary, Joseph's wife. Joseph believed in the angel, and the world benefited. Was Mrs. Merrill an angel from God, guiding him toward a destiny that he could never imagine? Why was she not surprised at his promotion? Was she indeed, his guiding angel? Whatever she was, his life would never again be the same as a result of meeting her.

CHAPTER TWENTY

One week after Jeff's conversation with Mrs. Merrill, Captain Kelly informed him that the battalion would embark for Europe within the next thirty days. A frenzy of activity followed this announcement. Medical records had to be updated, inoculations, last wills and testaments, new uniforms and other things had to be attended to.

The mood of the company was sometimes somber, but always confident. They had trained hard for twelve long weeks in the expectation that this day would come. Now the day was here and they were ready. Captain Kelly said he was proud of them. He told them that he had every reason to believe that their mission to Europe would be successful.

The day the company boarded the train for the long trip to the New York port of embarkation, there was a mood of calm resignation. When all of the troops were settled in, Jeff went from coach to coach checking the official roster against the name of each man on the train. When he was satisfied that all were present and accounted for, he reported his findings to Captain Kelly and the train eased its way out of the station toward New York.

The rumble of the train and the clickity clack of the tracks made weird sounds. Jeff desperately wanted to sleep but as hard as he tried, sleep eluded him. Each time he thought he had crossed over the threshold between being awake and falling asleep, something from his past entered his consciousness and sleep escaped him again.

His mind drifted back to almost two years ago. The events that brought him to the Army and onto this train were vividly framed in his consciousness. When he was six, the Klan had come to get his father. The years between that time and his running away to enlist had been hard. There was little opportunity to attend school and often too little to eat. His family moved often because they could not always earn enough money to pay the rent. His family, like all black families in the South, were segregated and forced to exist under what were sometimes subhuman conditions. Now, he sat on a train headed for New York where he would be shipped across the ocean to help liberate Europe, a continent he had never even had an opportunity to read about as he grew up in rural Alabama.

"What's wrong with this picture?" Jeff thought. Was the camera out of focus and his perception obscured or was there a more serious problem here? Whatever the problem was, his present duty was clear.

His lies about the enlistment had been forgiven. Some very powerful officers had reached out to give him a helping hand and his life and his family's life were better because of these events. In exchange for his liberation from the oppression he had endured, he was willing to be a part of the liberation of a continent he knew almost nothing about.

With Mrs. Merrill's help, he had carefully read the Constitution of the United States. She had said that one day soon, every section of this country and all of its people would have to live under and abide by this document. Maybe this journey was a long first step in that direction.

Sitting in the dark train, where most of the passengers were sleeping, Jeff could vividly recall the dialogue between Mrs. Merrill and himself. When she explained to him how the Constitution was constructed and what it was designed to do, he was more convinced than ever that the Constitution did not apply to him or to any other black person. He said as much to Mrs. Merrill.

She was incensed at his remarks. She brushed back her long blond hair, cleared her throat and focused her deep blue eyes directly upon him. Her voice trembled as she spoke.

"Now you hear me, Jeff. You hear me good. This document applies to me, to you and to every other citizen of this land. The fact that some people would have you believe that it does not apply to you is wrong. If you continue to believe that this document excludes you, then you do nothing but play into the hands of those bigots."

"Believing is one thing, Mrs. Merrill," Jeff pressed, "but what can I do to act on my beliefs? How can I make my beliefs come alive?"

"By doing just what you're doing now," she said. "You're a member of the Armed Forces of the United States. You volunteered. The fact that you're willing to risk your life for a cause that this country holds dear shows your loyalty. This loyalty simply cannot go unrecognized.

"This war won't last forever. All wars eventually come to an end. When it's over, this country and its people will never again be the same. When you go home after the war is over, continue to educate yourself, just as you've done here with me. When you've done that, decide within yourself what it is you'd like to see changed. Organize and move forward.

"Always bear in mind that freedom has a price tag. If you're willing to pay the price, you can acquire this precious commodity," she concluded.

As an afterthought she said, "You're as free as you think you are."

After many long hours, the train reached New York. A flurry of activity took place in the staging area before the men boarded the small liberty ship bound for England. Captain Kelly briefed the company officers and First Sergeant Wiggins about what to expect upon arrival in England.

"The voyage," said the captain, "takes seven to nine days. Because of the size of the ship, it's anticipated that a large number of soldiers will become seasick. Encourage as many men as possible to spend time on the deck where the cold fresh air from the North Atlantic may help alleviate seasickness."

As they crossed the ocean, Jeff and the other noncommissioned officers circulated in the areas where the troops were billeted to ascertain their condition and to get medical help where needed. Jeff reported the condition of the troops to the captain and the other officers twice daily. Jeff, along with the members of the company, looked forward to setting foot on dry land again.

When they finally docked in Scotland, the men departed the ship with renewed respect for the Navy. The company disembarked into a holding area. The weather in Scotland was bitter cold. The holding area was bursting at its seams with thousands of troops from all branches of the military services. Captain Kelly informed the company that they would be transported to London by train the following day. From there, they moved to a training area at a place called Westbury Wilts.

Westbury Wilts was a small camp that had, at some period, housed a British garrison. The company was quickly settled and almost immediately started on a rigorous program that would prepare them for whatever support mission the higher authorities had in mind. Captain Kelly informed Jeff, off the record, that there was talk among the higher echelon of a landing on the coast of France. The captain had no further details but the type of training that the company was undergoing tended to support the idea that the company would be a part of some hostile action.

Captain Kelly inspected the troops more often than usual and his mood was more somber than it had ever been. His attitude and his mood told the company that this was not business as usual. Captain Kelly spoke often about the need to be so highly trained that, if there were casualties, they would be kept to a minimum. Jeff knew the captain well. He could anticipate his moods as well as his decisions.

There was very little time to think or reflect. But when there were such moments, Jeff would use them to look back over the events of the past three years. The events that led up to where he now found himself always came to his mind. He thought about Sergeant Faulkner, the recruiting sergeant who had enlisted him. He also thought about the board of officers, Captain O'Hara, and especially, the general. Somehow all of these people were pieces of a puzzle that represented his life.

Jeff only began to understand how these pieces came together when he met Mrs. Merrill. She had frequently said that we all would like to believe that we are independent entities, when in fact we are quite interdependent. We draw strength, wisdom, and ambition from each other. She said that wherever our journey takes us, it's good for all of us to remember that someone, some group of people, helped us get there.

It all seemed very clear now. Jeff saw himself in this foreign country that seemed so far away two or three short years ago. He had more responsibility now than most people would have in a lifetime. He clearly realized that he did not get here solely by his own doing. The actions of Sergeant Faulkner, Captain O'Hara, Mama Essie, the JAG, the board of officers and the general all seemed to come together—and those actions had catapulted him to this place.

Mama Essie had said to the general, when he was speaking to her about allowing Jeff to remain in the Army, that soldiers get injured and sometimes die. The general had agreed, but he said those soldiers who were killed died with honor. Jeff was not a voluntary candidate for death but he realized that the three years that he had been in the Army were the best years of his life.

Unlike his father, Jeff did not have to worry about or be afraid of the KKK. He did not have to grow up and still be called a 'boy'. In the Army, he was respected for his character and his achievement, no matter his color. To him, the risk of dying in this foreign land was better than the relative safety of his life in the dehumanizing society of his hometown. In all wars, there were survivors and, in this war, Jeff intended to be one of them.

In early May, Captain Kelly informed the company that it had been placed on alert and would be moved to a staging area near Portsmouth, England. Although the unit had expected to move, reality did not set in until the captain's announcement. Captain Kelly assured the company that they would remain intact and that he had full confidence in the unit. He said that he considered it a privilege to be the commander of such dedicated soldiers. Over a cup of coffee in the mess hall, the captain complimented Jeff for getting the men ready for this important move. He said, "First Sergeant, no matter what happens, I will always be proud of you. You beat the odds and came off the winner. You are a survivor."

Portsmouth was organized chaos, or so it seemed—hundreds of thousands of men and supplies, vehicles of every description, trunks, tanks, artillery pieces and so much more. Captain Kelly and the other officers kept close watch over the company and tried to keep morale high during these trying times. There was little to do during these times except, as the Army liked to say, "Hurry up and wait."

Jeff and the platoon sergeants spent the daylight hours reassuring each soldier that their training, their superior equipment, and the leadership of Captain Kelly would serve them well, no matter what they encountered. One soldier approached Jeff and said, "First Sergeant, I need to talk."

Jeff had always been impressed with this soldier's performance. He was quiet, almost introverted, but he was quick to grasp new challenges and to understand what was expected of him. This soldier was several years older than Jeff, but he always held Jeff up as a model soldier.

"Can you and I take a walk, First Sergeant?" the soldier asked.

"I suppose we could but with all the troops and equipment all over the place, where can we walk?" Jeff said.

They walked a few feet to a place where a group of medics was stretched out on the ground, sleeping. Jeff looked directly into the soldier's eyes. "I'm ready to talk."

"First Sergeant," the soldier began, "what's going to happen to us?"

"I don't know soldier," Jeff said.

"Where are we going?"

"To France," Jeff said. "We're just a few miles from the coast of France now."

"When will we be leaving?"

"I don't know that for sure," Jeff replied, "but with all of these men and equipment here, it has to be soon."

"I'm scared, First Sergeant," the soldier said. "Are you?"

"Yes, I am soldier. I am very scared."

"What are you going to do?"

"I'm going to do exactly what I have been trained to do and so are you."

Tears began to stream down the soldier's face. His body shook and he had great difficulty speaking.

"Are you ashamed of me, First Sergeant?" the soldier pleaded.

"No, soldier, I'm not ashamed of you. I'm proud of you."

"What is there to be proud of, First Sergeant? I'm a coward, falling apart like this."

Jeff could sympathize with this soldier because he knew what fear could do to a person. He knew the kind of fear this soldier was feeling. The summer night that the KKK came for his father brought him almost paralyzing fear. The one thing that relieved him of this temporary fear was his family's move to another county. They ran away from the scene of the fear. It was vastly different in the matter facing this soldier. He could not run away to the next county. He had to control his fear another way.

"It takes a brave man to admit fear," Jeff told the soldier. "Just admitting that you're scared goes a long way toward conquering your fear."

"A certain amount of fear is healthy," Jeff continued. "It tells you to be vigilant, to be on guard, to protect yourself at all times and to protect those around you. Don't get careless, and, most of all, remember your training. Captain Kelly is a good officer, a tremendous leader. I suspect that there's a little fear in him also."

"You won't tell the captain how scared I am, will you, First Sergeant?"

"No, soldier," Jeff assured him. "This conversation never took place as far as I am concerned."

CHAPTER TWENTY-ONE

Within twenty-four hours, the weather at Portsmouth turned foul. The clouds and fog moved in and the rains came, accompanied by strong winds. The ships in the harbor swayed under the force of relentless waves. Captain Kelly instructed the company to stay together and be ready to move out on his command.

Loaded on the ship, sitting in the channel, the anxiety among the troops continued to build. It was still fog shrouded, windy, and cold. The ship left the port for what everyone thought was one of the beaches of France. In fact, after a short sail, the ship dropped anchor in what seemed like the middle of the channel. The storm had intensified and the ship rocked relentlessly under heavy attack from the waves that had been kicked up by the brutal storm. The captain, the company officers and Jeff monitored the condition of the men in the company. They put on their best faces in the presence of the troops, but they found that the majority of the troops were now seasick. Jeff approached the soldier who had told him how scared he was.

"How do you feel, soldier?" Jeff asked.

"I feel a lot better now, First Sergeant," was his reply. "I'm still scared, but I prayed with the chaplain and I'm resigned to the fact that God is just not ready for me now. You don't need to worry about me, First Sergeant. I'll do my duty just as I've been trained to do. I imagine a few Germans are not supermen. They're soldiers like you, me and the rest of the troops. They bleed and die, too."

For hours, the storm over the channel intensified. The condition of the men in the company seemed to worsen. The medical personnel were kept busy. Those who were not seasick were depressed because of the severe storm. After fourteen hours, Captain Kelly informed the company that when the storm receded the

ship would get under way again. It would drop anchor as close to
Normandy beach as it could get. The company would disembark
the ship on landing crafts that would transport them within a few
feet of the beach. He cautioned the men to hit the beach as quickly
as possible, to dig in and to wait for instructions from the officers.

"First Sergeant," the captain said, "you go ashore in the first
wave and be alert for the remainder of the company. Stay alert.
Good first sergeants are hard to come by."

The ship dropped anchor two to three hundred yards from
the beach. The landing craft swiftly moved alongside the ship. Jeff
elected to descend the rope ladder first. He wanted to be on the
beach when the bulk of the company arrived. Captain Kelly agreed
that this was a good move.

The powerful engines of the landing craft continued to roar as
the men quickly descended. Captain Kelly and the company officers
supervised the landing. The company executive officer was the last
to descend the ladder and he directed the craft to head for the
beach. It was still overcast and it seemed that there was a slight
drizzle but it was hard to be certain because the powerful motors
from the landing craft, combined with the strong wind, sent plumes
of water all over the place.

Jeff motioned to the men to adjust their field packs and to
make sure that their rifles remained as dry as possible. In a matter
of moments, the landing craft began moving at breakneck speed,
headed for the beach. Within a few seconds, the craft was as close
as it could get to shore. The gate of the vessel fell forward and the
men scrambled off, into the waste-deep, bone-chilling water. They
moved swiftly toward the damp sand. Lieutenant Anderson moved
alongside Jeff and said the platoon should continue to move forward,
if possible, another hundred yards. The soldier who had talked
about his fear a few days before moved swiftly past Jeff. He looked
back with a wide grin on his face and said, "Welcome to France,
First Sergeant."

Within the next twenty minutes, the entire company was on
the lower part of the beach. Captain Kelly directed the company
to dig in and wait for orders from him. On the hill above,

approximately a thousand yards away, fierce fighting was taking place between fortified German gun emplacements and well-equipped American infantry divisions. Hitler's vaunted Atlantic wall had been penetrated, but at a devastating price to the Americans.

For the first few hours, the company did not move forward. They remained dug in, shivering in wet uniforms and wondering what would be next. The German artillery continued to lob shell after shell into the channel, where hundreds of ships and other small vessels were anchored. The beach and the channel were littered with dead and wounded soldiers. Captain Kelly was in communication with battalion headquarters. He informed the company officers and Jeff that the American forces were stalled because of lack of air support.

"It had been predicted," the captain explained "that the ceiling would lift within a few hours and that air support would be out in force. For now," the captain concluded, "just have the men 'hurry up and wait'."

Crawling on the wet sand, Jeff spoke to each platoon leader. He relayed the captain's messages, told the sergeants that, except for a broken leg and a fractured knee, the company had suffered no major casualties.

Captain Kelly ordered Jeff to remain as close to him as possible. "I'll need you to calm a few nerves if the situation turns ugly on the beach."

Jeff lost track of time. The minutes seemed to drag and the hours stood still. At some point, Captain Kelly moved in close to Jeff and said, "First Sergeant, do you hear anything?"

"I hear small arms, mortar, and artillery fire, sir," Jeff said.

"Look back, First Sergeant. Look out over the channel."

As Jeff looked, he heard a sound that was as soothing to him as the old-time hymns he used to hear when his Grandma Dawson took him to her small country church. What he heard was the drone of aircraft in the distance. The company was so fatigued and so happy to be alive, they had barely noticed that the ceiling had lifted considerably and that the sun was peeking through. Out over the horizon appeared what looked to him like a huge flock of black birds. But he knew that birds didn't make those kinds of sounds. Wave after wave of American fighter planes that seemed to have risen out of the choppy channel flew overhead. Wherever he looked, planes filled the sky.

Within seconds, the planes swooped over the German gun positions—strafing, dropping bombs, and creating havoc for the Germans. Heavy bombers followed closely behind the fighter planes. Bombs rained down on the German positions. The earth seemed to shake under the intense, relentless attack. Jeff looked up to see this vast armada of machines overhead. Despite the danger involved in this action, the morale of the troops on the beaches soared as each bomb exploded over the German positions. The fabled Atlantic wall, the pride of the Third Reich, was not just pierced; the wall was forever destroyed. The Allied forces pushed across France with deliberate speed and it seemed, at first, that the collapse of the German Army was only a matter of weeks away.

Five months after living through death-dealing scenes on the beach where they had first landed, Captain Kelly informed Jeff and the company that they had been ordered to take up a position in preparation for being deployed wherever support services were needed. Being part of a long truck convoy moving from central France to the Belgian border was a relief from what the company had experienced on the ground during and after the invasion. For the first time in weeks, they experienced relief from the constant pressure of trying to survive.

Captain Kelly spoke to the company en masse for the first time since landing on the beach. His words were pointed and sincere. He told the company how extremely proud he was of their performance. He said that he could visualize the day, in the not-too-distant future, when they would board another ship and sail home.

As the convoy rumbled over the French countryside, Jeff's thoughts were not on Belgium but were, once again, on the past. He recalled the conversation between his mother, Mama Essie, and the general back at Fort Wadsworth. Mama Essie had told the general that her biggest objection to Jeff remaining in the Army was the possibility of his death in battle. The general had understood her concern, but said that if this occurred, it would be with honor, an honor that may or not be the reality for a runaway son. Reluctantly, Mama Essie had accepted this reasoning and her decision had changed Jeff's life.

Seated in the jeep at the head of the convoy as it moved toward Belgium, Jeff knew in his heart how much he was indebted to so many people, but especially to Mama Essie. It seemed to him that the actions taken by these people had made possible all of the good things that had happened to him up to this point in his young life.

As the jeep rocked and rolled along the countryside, Jeff tried to get some much-needed sleep, but sleep would not come. Lingering in the deep recesses of his mind was his anger at not being able to recall anything about his early life. What were the first few years of his life like? He should have recalled something, but try as he might, Jeff could remember nothing of his life before the night the Klan came.

How was it, he thought, that he could remember in minute detail most of the things that occurred after that event, but not one thing that occurred before? As matters stood, his conscious life began when he was six years old. He seemed to have only six years in his life which could correctly be called "childhood". As a teenager, he had declared himself an adult and illegally entered the United States Army. The Army had accepted him as a man and they treated him like a man. Jeff wondered what it would have been like to grow up as a child, to be able to recall something of your childhood. It did not matter that the childhood memories might have been painful and hard. He needed to have the memories to make his present life complete.

During a fifteen-minute break in the trip toward the Belgian border, Captain Kelly approached him. "First Sergeant, are you all right? You look as if you have just encountered a ghost from your past. I've never seen such a look on you."

Jeff had no idea that he had been so shaken by his own thoughts.

"Captain," he said, "I've been trying to make contact with a few ghosts from my past, but they've eluded me."

After the break ended, Jeff was determined that he would put these things out of his mind for now, but these heart-wrenching thoughts would not leave him. Was there someone, some place, something that would help him to reclaim the memory of this vital part of his life? He had heard and read that hypnosis could help recapture lost memory. Was this a resource that could help him? It was painful not being able to at least fill that void in his life. At this point, he was willing to seek help wherever he could find it.

He did recall that Grandma Dawson had once told him a story about his name. She said, "The name you now have is not the name you always had. There was a dispute between your father's family and your mother's family about what name to give you. Your father wanted to name you 'Clarence', the name of his brother. Your mother objected. She wanted to name you 'Henry', after her brother. The dispute couldn't be resolved, so they named you 'Scott' and you kept that name until you were four years old. Your mother," Grandma Dawson said, "was not satisfied and so, when you were four years old, she wrote to the Bureau of Vital Statistics at Montgomery and had your name legally changed to 'Jefferson'. Your father never liked the name, and so he gave you a nickname. He called you 'Woodly'."

Jeff had often wondered if the hassle over his name had anything to do with his lost memory. He didn't know, but Jefferson was much more to his liking than Scott, Clarence, Henry, or Woodly.

The convoy arrived in Belgium after dark. For the moment, the flurry of activity involved in getting settled into this new station did not permit these thoughts to continue tormenting him.

The weather was beginning to change drastically. The days were sunny but the nights were cold. Captain Kelly took every opportunity available to him to remind the company that they were only a few miles from the German border and that the war was not yet over. He reminded the unit to remain vigilant.

The company was billeted in a small school building and

waited for its new assignment from headquarters. Jeff was a world away from his brief childhood in Alabama. He wondered how his parents had endured the inhuman treatment to which they had been subjected over their lifetime, treatment that was worse than even he had ever known.

Grandma Dawson had, at times, commented on her life of oppression, a life with no hope of relief. She was born in 1872, just a few short years after the Emancipation Proclamation. Jeff's grandfather, who was ten years older than Grandma Dawson, had been born into slavery. Grandma Dawson reasoned that, as precious as freedom was, one could never fully appreciate a freedom that they had never known. Jeff knew that he would have to respectfully disagree with Grandma Dawson. From the time of his first memory, he was actually aware that there were almost slave-like restrictions placed upon him. He was not free to go to school if there was work to be done; he was not free to express his feelings and opinions to white people; he was not free to protest the restrictions placed upon all black people.

There were "colored" waiting rooms in the bus and train stations and separate educational facilities for those blacks who were lucky enough to attend school. There were severe sanctions for anyone who violated these restrictions. Jeff's father knew this only too well. His violation of the landowner's rules was regarded as a sign of rebelliousness for which the ultimate sanction was almost extracted.

Now, Jeff reasoned, here he was, the grandson of a former slave, far away from the land of his birth, fighting for the freedom of a nation that was not his own. What did it all mean? Jeff supposed that it meant that those who had never been totally free could still understand the plight of those who had known freedom and lost it.

Three days after the company's arrival in Belgium, their assignment came down from headquarters. Jeff and Captain Kelly were unprepared for the assignment they received. They were to work with a graves registration company. Essentially, this meant that, after the graves registration experts properly identified a soldier who had been killed in the field, their unit was to prepare a proper burial. This included digging graves and burying the bodies.

To Jeff and most of the men in the company, this duty was the most depressing they had ever been called upon to perform. Sure, they had seen many bodies on the beach and in the water of the channel, but this was different. With this assignment, the men would have to touch the bodies and give them an appropriate burial in accordance with the religious practices of the deceased.

Emotionally, it was draining. The company buried an average of two hundred bodies a day. The cemetery was divided into two sections—one section for Americans and the other section for the German dead. Near the end of November, the company officers noted that fewer Americans were brought in for burial, but German bodies were coming at a five-to-one ratio compared to American bodies. Captain Kelly asked Jeff his thoughts about this change.

"I would guess, sir," Jeff said, "that the American fire power is taking its toll on the German Army."

The captain agreed. "The German Army," he said, "knows it's about to be knocked out and it's looking for a place to fall."

More and more, the bodies of the German dead seemed too young to be those of soldiers. Every few days, a few German women were brought into the cemetery for burial.

By late November, the company had settled in to its job of burying the American and German dead. The job was no more pleasant than it had been at the beginning. But it was a necessary job. It had to be done. Each member of the company was extremely impressed with the care that the experts in the graves registration company used to identify each body before burial. It was painstaking work, carried out with dignity and sensitivity.

Captain Kelly talked more often now about going home to the United States. He believed that it would only be a few days before the American troops would move into Germany and force the Germans to fight on their home soil. Daily raids by the Air Force had reduced Germany's industrial complex to rubble and their ground forces were in full retreat. In spite of the grim task of burying the dead each day, morale within the company was high. Each soldier now felt that the war was almost over and a homecoming was not too far in the future.

Headquarters had begun to issue liquor and beer rations and there was an air of conquest among the troops in the area. The third platoon sergeant had organized a gospel group and they entertained the company nightly. Sergeant Culver always sang Jeff's favorite song, "Nobody Knows the Trouble I've Seen".

One cold, rainy night, the sergeant asked, "First Sergeant, you always have us sing that song for you. Why?"

"I don't really know," Jeff replied, "except that the words take me back to where I came from."

Jeff did know why he especially liked this song. He had learned it from his mother. When things were going badly, Mama Essie would break out in song. When he was younger, Jeff did not fully understand what it meant to her, but as he grew older he gradually began to understand. Mama Essie was a mild-mannered, deeply religious woman. She always denied herself in order that her family could have more of whatever scarce commodities they had. Her children were always given the largest helping of food. She made shirts and trousers for her boys from old bedsheets and other materials that were given to her. She never complained, but sometimes late at night, Jeff could hear her in prayer. She asked God's protection for her family. Jeff could never recall a time when he heard her ask for anything for herself.

Clemon Wiggins

Mama Essie

First Lieutenant Jefferson Wiggins

Photo by Carol Kaliff, The News-Times
Jefferson and Janice Wiggins

CHAPTER TWENTY-TWO

In early December, the company got orders to move from its location near Liege and to proceed about twenty miles southeast to a village between Liege and Bastogne. Upon the company's arrival, they began to hear wild rumors of a major German offensive that was about to be launched. The weather was miserable; it was snowing and overcast, with bone-chilling winds. Captain Kelly was in a foul mood because the company had left relatively comfortable quarters for this windswept, snow-filled village. Over the next two to three days, the company settled into several vacant shell-damaged buildings. An orderly room, mess hall and communications center were set up and in operation. The rumors of a large German offensive continued to surface.

The company intelligence officer spoke to a Flemish-speaking family from Bastogne. They told him of large German troop movements not too far from their village. The intelligence officer passed this information on to the higher echelons, as required. In daily jeep drives around the area, Captain Kelly told the company officers and Jeff that he had an ominous feeling that something was in the air. It was too quiet, the captain said. It was only a short time before Christmas, but he sensed that this was an eerie kind of quiet.

Two nights after his remarks, the captain and three of the company officers came into the orderly room and the captain said, "First Sergeant, we're going to reconnoiter the area, would you care to come along?"

"I'd like to, sir, but I'm preparing a report for your signature that's due at battalion headquarters at o-eight hundred hours tomorrow."

The jeep carrying the officers left. With the report finished, Jeff told the charge of quarters to wake him when the captain and the other officers returned. Fully dressed, Jeff fell into a deep sleep. At 0400, the CQ woke Jeff to tell him that the captain and the officers had not returned. Alarmed, Jeff's first thoughts were to inform the battalion commander. He placed a call to headquarters and spoke to the duty officer. Jeff explained the circumstances and asked that the colonel be informed immediately. The duty officer insisted that the colonel could not be disturbed. "The captain is an astute officer; he knows how to take care of himself."

"Lieutenant," Jeff answered, "what you just said is my problem. The captain does know how to take care of himself. But he would never remain away from the company this long under ordinary circumstances. Would you like your duty roster, your report, to show that I placed this call at o-four twelve hours?"

"Your concern is noted, First Sergeant. Don't panic."

At 0435, the colonel called Jeff. "Have they returned, First Sergeant?"

"No, sir, I've heard nothing."

"This is serious stuff, First Sergeant," the colonel said. "How's your security there?"

"It's adequate under the present conditions," Jeff said.

"First Sergeant, call me every hour on the hour until we know more about this situation than we now know," the colonel ordered.

At 0452, the colonel called again. Jeff worried about this call because the colonel's tone had changed; his worry and concerns were clearly reflected in his voice.

"First Sergeant," he said, "extend the perimeters of your security by three hundred yards and double the number of men you have out there."

"Yes, sir," Jeff answered. "Colonel, is there something else I should know?"

"Yes, there is," the colonel said. "You're authorized to shoot to kill anyone who attempts to breach your security."

Jeff ordered the charge of quarters to wake up and summon the platoon sergeants to his office immediately. The platoon sergeants were excited about this new turn of events. They had been through this enhanced security procedure before and they

fully understood what they had to do. The company was assembled
in a small courtyard adjoining one of the buildings. Jeff gave them
as much information as he had, which was not very much
information at all. The security was doubled and the perimeters
extended. Now the waiting game began.

At 0710, the colonel came to the company to see if anything
had been heard from the four officers.

The colonel spoke rapidly, and stared Jeff in the eye. "First
Sergeant, we have a very serious and crucial situation developing
all around us. In a few hours, the main thoroughfare will be
cluttered with heavy military hardware moving up to engage the
German offensive. There's been a massive breach of our lines all
along the front. The war's not yet over. Keep your men on alert
and at full readiness. Someone from my headquarters will keep
you informed of the things you need to know. Do you have
questions?"

"Just one question, sir," Jeff replied. "When will the colonel
assign new officers to the company?"

"First Sergeant, that's a question I had hoped you wouldn't
ask. I have no officers to assign at this time. I've requested officers
from regiment, but, under the present circumstances, I don't
anticipate that any will be coming in the short run. You're it, First
Sergeant. Use your platoon sergeants to your best advantage. You
have a well-disciplined company. You're a top-of-the-line first
sergeant. You know what has to be done and you know how to get
it done."

Jeff felt like the weight of the world had been dropped on his
shoulders. It was one matter to help Captain Kelly formulate plans,
to assist him in making wise decisions, but it was another matter
now that the decisions were his alone to make.

"Dammit, Captain, why did you and all of the company officers
have to go off in that jeep and leave us here alone?"

A thousand thoughts were running through Jeff's mind and
many of them made him angry. He knew that anger was the last
thing he needed to have to deal with right now. There were more
important things to do. Just as the colonel had said, the roads were

jammed with every type of military hardware moving up to engage the German armies. Heavy tanks, long- and short-range artillery, elite infantry foot soldiers, hospital units and more. In addition, the roads were crowded with refugees who were once again fleeing the onslaught of the German Army.

Jeff had instructed his platoon sergeants to use their men to keep the roads clear in order for the advancing Americans to move with deliberate speed. The weather was not cooperating with the Americans. It was snowing steadily and the Army Air Force could not fly because of the low ceiling.

It had now been five days since Captain Kelly and the other company officers had left in a jeep. Everyone was resigned to the fact that the worst had happened and they would more than likely never return. The colonel checked on the company daily and he told Jeff that he was very proud of the performance of the unit. Each man in the company bent over backwards to give Jeff his best. They were like family.

The buildup on the roads was at its peak now. Jeff had not seen this much military hardware since their days on the beach at Normandy. It was clear to him that whatever was happening, it was big time.

The weather did not get any better. It remained extremely cold and windy. The blowing snow made it difficult for vehicles on the clogged roads to travel. The colonel ordered Jeff to have the company ready to move out at 0500 the following morning. The battalion, he said, would take up a position a few miles south of Bastogne. The move began smoothly, but the nearer the battalion got to Bastogne, the clearer it became that fierce fighting was taking place between the American and German armies. Heavy artillery and mortar fire could be heard in the distance. Wounded American soldiers could be seen as they were evacuated from the front lines. The colonel placed the battalion in a defensive holding position and he told them to be ready for any type of attack.

The company headquarters was located in an abandoned barn. Sitting in the barn just before noon, Jeff was going over some reports when two soldiers rushed in, excited and out of breath.

"First Sergeant," one soldier shouted, "you're not going to believe who's outside and headed in here."

"Settle down, soldier," Jeff ordered. Before he could speak further, into the barn walked a rather small man, surrounded by heavy security and escorted by a captain and a full colonel. His shiny helmet gleamed with three silver stars and he wore two pearl-handled pistols on his gun belt.

Jeff jumped to his feet, rushed to meet the general and stopped to render a smart salute. In his entire military career, Jeff had never been this nervous and excited, but because of his good training in military protocol and discipline, he knew instinctively what to do. Jeff stood at rigid attention as the general walked to the side, to the back and returned to the front to face Jeff.

"Are you a real first sergeant?" the general demanded.

To this point, Jeff had said nothing. He knew that you did not speak to a general unless he spoke to you first.

"Yes, sir," Jeff said. "I am a real first sergeant."

"You look damn young to me. How old are you, First Sergeant?"

Jeff's mind and mouth were frozen. He couldn't even remember how to speak.

"Get your company commander in here," the general ordered.

Jeff quickly came to his senses. "We have no company commander, sir, nor do we have officers."

"Are you telling me you're the ranking man in this outfit, First Sergeant?"

"I am, sir."

The colonel briefly explained to the general the circumstances surrounding the missing officers.

"Colonel," the general said, "this is a perfect example of the caliber of soldier this country can produce. This soldier and millions like him enable me to kick kraut asses all over Europe—and I'm not finished yet."

"Yes, sir," the colonel replied.

During this brief exchange between the general and the colonel, Jeff had just enough time to realize that he was standing in the presence of a legend. General George S. Patton was known around the world as one of America's greatest and most colorful generals. The very thought increased Jeff's excitement.

Suddenly, the general looked squarely into Jeff's eyes. He didn't seem to blink. The voice of the general seemed to drop an octave and he said, "First Sergeant, I believe you would make an outstanding officer. I think I may give you a direct field commission. What is your reaction to my thoughts?"

"Can I think about it, sir?" Jeff asked nervously.

"What the hell is there to think about, soldier?" the general scolded Jeff. "Too much thought leads to hesitation. But since you need to think, I'll give you thirty seconds."

"I defer to the general," Jeff said.

"Get me the necessary information, Colonel."

"Yes, sir," the colonel said. The colonel took Jeff's name, rank, and serial number and, as quickly as they came, they were gone.

Jeff looked at his watch. The visit had lasted less than five minutes. Five minutes and his life, once again, seemed on the verge of drastic change. He had never entertained the idea of becoming a commissioned officer. During his military career, he had met and served with some outstanding officers—some from West Point, some from ROTC programs at outstanding colleges, many from officers candidate school. All were good officers, but that was for them. Jeff knew that he was at the highest enlisted grade that he could achieve in the military. He was proud of what he had been able to accomplish, but he was also quick to realize how much luck and timing had played in his favor. He was an enlisted man and his thoughts and actions were that of an enlisted man. Now this famous general had taken over his life for a few brief minutes and all of this was about to change.

It was mind boggling. How would he act as a newly commissioned officer? Would he have to leave this company that he loved so much? Word of the general's visit spread quickly throughout the company and the battalion. The men of his company were beside themselves with pride. Previously hidden bottles of schnapps, cognac, calvados and a few bottles of Bottled in Bond suddenly appeared to facilitate a toast from members of the company in honor of Jeff.

"Hold it, gentlemen," admonished Jeff. "The deed is not yet done. I'm still one of you. I'm still an enlisted man." Jeff knew that this was, perhaps, the last time he would be able to have a drink with them.

Five days passed before Jeff was summoned to the general's headquarters. Upon his arrival, a brigadier general and a full colonel appeared in the sparsely furnished room with maps spread out over makeshift tables. Telephone lines were twisted everywhere.

The colonel ceremoniously removed the first sergeant stripes. The general pinned two gold bars on Jeff's field jacket and another gold bar on his shirt collar. The general shook hands with Jeff and gave him a hearty "Congratulations!"

Jeff stepped back, saluted and said, "Thank you, sir." The transition from enlisted man to officer was complete.

"Is there anything else we can do for you, Lieutenant?" the colonel inquired.

"Yes, sir, there is," Jeff said. "Would the colonel be kind enough to give me back my old first sergeant stripes?"

"Are you going to give them to your first grandson?" the colonel asked.

"No, sir," Jeff replied. "I am going to give them to the man who replaces me as first sergeant."

The general and the colonel returned to their offices. The driver who brought Jeff to the general's headquarters was waiting downstairs. When Jeff appeared, ready for the nine-mile drive back to his company, the driver looked at Jeff and glanced at the shiny gold bars. He jumped to his feet, saluted and said, "Congratulations, sir, we did it. We made history." Jeff had never seen a black officer in his entire Army career. He doubted that any of the men in his company had either. Now he was one. He knew very well what the driver's words meant.

"Thank you, soldier," Jeff replied. "Now see to it that you get me back to the company before this dream ends."

On the road headed back to battalion headquarters and to his own company, Jeff thought about the words the soldier uttered when he first saw the gold bars on his shoulders. "We did it, sir."

How appropriate. Jeff was deeply grateful for the way his company had performed for the entire time they had been in Europe. What the soldier's words had said to him was, "Your success is our success. We support you for your leadership and you support us for our good performance."

As the jeep moved along the snow-covered road, Jeff's thoughts drifted back to the morning he had slipped away from home to join the Army and to the day of the hearing at Fort Wadsworth after he had confessed his true age. Mama Essie, the board of officers—led by the JAG—and the general had all played a hand in getting him to this place. Mrs. Merrill had played no small role in educating him and getting him to understand the value of learning. More than ever, he knew that all of these people and the power that compelled them had joined together to bring about this day.

Jeff knew that he was required to report in to battalion headquarters upon his arrival. What he did not know was that the general at Patton's Headquarters had informed the battalion commander about his commission and that Jeff and the driver were on their way back to battalion headquarters. As Jeff entered the building, it seemed strange to him that only the sentry on guard at the entrance was visible. Suddenly, all of the headquarters personnel, led by the colonel, rushed in and shouted their congratulations. The colonel held a ceremonial bottle of French champagne. He dismissed the headquarters personnel and spoke directly to Jeff.

"Lieutenant," he said, "I'm proud of you and I'm proud of your men. As I told you a few days ago, I have no junior grade officers to assign to your company. Therefore, I'm assigning you as company commander. You have my complete support in whatever you need. I know you must have a few questions. Fire away."

"I suppose, sir," Jeff began, "that my highest priority is selecting a new first sergeant."

"Send me your recommendation and I'll approve it," said the battalion commander. "But remember, Lieutenant, that whoever we promote to first sergeant creates three other vacancies. Let's fill them all on the same order."

"Yes, sir," Jeff replied.

"I'll go with you back to your company," the colonel said. "I'd like to introduce the men to their new commanding officer."

The company was assembled in the small mess hall when the colonel arrived with Jeff. The adjutant was present as well as the battalion executive officer. As they entered the room, the senior platoon sergeant called the company to attention. He then approached the colonel. "Staff Sergeant Marcus Anderson reporting, sir."

"Don't report to me, Sergeant," the colonel said. "Report to your new commanding officer."

The sergeant then stepped directly in front of Jeff. He saluted smartly and said, "Sir, Staff Sergeant Marcus Anderson proudly reports to the new company commander."

Staff Sergeant Anderson stood before Jeff, waiting for his salute to be returned. Tears of pride streamed down Anderson's face, despite his attempt to hold them back.

Jeff returned his salute and said, "Sergeant, take your post with the remainder of the company."

Jeff said simply, "As you were, gentlemen."

One soldier in the front of the group shouted, "May I speak, sir?"

"You may speak, soldier."

"Sir," shouted the soldier, "how does the lieutenant expect us to be as we were under these circumstances? We'll never be as we were. We have one of our own as our leader."

The room exploded with shouts and applause. The noncommissioned officers of the company had difficulty restoring a sense of decorum. The colonel stopped forward and told the sergeants, "Let them celebrate, this is a day that they're not likely to see again."

Jeff understood the pride and the emotions in the room. That was the first time these black men had ever seen a black officer in the United States Army. They felt that they had helped to create this moment and that they had a right to celebrate. Jeff shared their feelings. Indeed, by their performance, they had made this moment possible.

The battalion commander and the adjutant stood in the background and smiled as this demonstration of unbridled support for Jeff continued. Finally, the two officers stepped forward. The battalion commander shook hands with Jeff and said, "Lieutenant, this is a great day, not just for you, but for all of us. It shows that integrity, determination and superior performance transcends whatever prejudices we have of each other. Celebrate the moment, you've earned it," he continued. "But I'm sure I don't need to remind you that less than twenty miles away, we're locked in a life-and-death struggle with the remnants of a desperate German Army."

The colonel and the adjutant departed as the platoon sergeants moved to bring some order to this wild demonstration. Now that Jeff was no longer the first sergeant, Staff Sergeant Marcus Anderson was the senior noncommissioned officer. In that capacity, he tried to bring order to the room. He told the men that each time they performed well would be a sign of their approval of what had happened today.

"The lieutenant is one of us and we intend to support his decisions," Sergeant Anderson continued. "Let's clean this room and return to our posts."

With order restored, Jeff summoned Staff Sergeant Anderson to a closed-door meeting in the corner of his tiny quarters.

"Sergeant," Jeff began, "you and I have some hard decisions to make. The biggest decision is the matter of a new first sergeant. I've chosen you," Jeff stated emphatically. "I need to hear your views and concerns. What are your thoughts, Sergeant?"

Anderson was silent for a moment. He then looked Jeff in the eyes and said, "Sir, your shoes will be hard to fill, but if I'm your choice, I'm up to the task."

"That's fine," Jeff said. "Now let's look at your replacement as platoon sergeant." An agreement for filling the vacancies created when Jeff was commissioned was quickly reached.

"Sergeant Anderson," Jeff instructed, "I want the company clerk to have the proper forms ready for my signature within the next two hours. You will personally deliver the papers to the battalion adjutant. And one other thing, Sergeant, the decisions we've made here will be kept under wraps until the new promotion list becomes official. Do you have questions or wish to say anything?"

"Yes, sir. I'd like to say that I appreciate the confidence you've placed in me and I'll do my best to justify that confidence," the sergeant concluded.

The battalion commander moved with deliberate speed to publish the orders of promotion. Within twenty-four hours, the promotions were confirmed. Jeff caused the company to be assembled and read the orders to them. They couldn't afford to have vacancies in the ranks. The fierce battle in and around Bastogne continued to rage. The colonel continued to hold the battalion in a support position, using a part of Jeff's unit to keep the supply lines open and to ensure the delivery of much needed supplies to depots near the front lines.

The weather was much improved and the low ceiling had lifted. American Air Force planes were all over the place—strafing, bombing and generally causing havoc to the German forces. Word soon came that the American forces had crossed the border into Germany. There was much talk about how long it would be before the total collapse of the German Army. That collapse and surrender came in May 1945.

CHAPTER TWENTY-THREE

In the days following the celebration throughout all of Europe, the commander was ordered to move the battalion into Germany. On the long convoy drive over roads where so much death and destruction had occurred over the last several months, an uneasy feeling came over Jeff. The beautiful countryside was now quiet and peaceful. As the convoy crossed the bridge over into Aachen, Germany, he was in awe of the magnificent cathedrals rising above the skyline of the city. Seeing these beautiful edifices in this city of cathedrals, Jeff wondered if, during the years leading up to the beginning of the war, the leaders of these churches had spoken out against the use of violence as a legitimate means of settling differences. Had the German clergy spoken out against genocide? During the course of the war, there were continuous reports of death camps, mass murders and forceful demonstrations of Aryan superiority over Jews and non-Germans. How, Jeff wondered, could the leaders and parishioners of all of these churches and cathedrals sit idly by? How could they fail to voice their disapproval of the brutal annihilations of people whose lives posed no armed threat to the country?

He was sensitive to acts of racism and violence. He had been born into and had lived much of his short life under a system of violence that was used to keep what Southern society considered to be the "less desirables" in a state of human servitude. Different continents, different countries, but he saw unsettling parallels.

The battalion's new station was a small village just northeast of Aachen. The weather was comfortable and there was no gunfire. First Sergeant Anderson found quarters for Jeff on the second floor of what had, until recently, been the home of a retired aircraft worker and his family. The home was comfortable and it afforded

Jeff the quietness he needed to sort through his thoughts. The war was over and thoughts of home were on the minds of just about everyone. What would he do, Jeff wondered, when he did finally get home? Would home be back in Alabama, the place he had run away from as a teenager, or would it be in some other place in another state? This was a decision he would have to make, but it was one he did not have to make today. Just as he was about to take a nap, the mail clerk brought his mail into his room.

"Sir," the mail clerk said, "you'd better write these people and tell them you're not a first sergeant any more. You're an officer and we want everyone to know it."

"Give them time, soldier, give them time," Jeff said. He knew that the men in the company were still bursting with pride because one of their own was their commander. Jeff examined the stack of letters carefully. This was the first mail the battalion had received in weeks. With the Battle of the Bulge being fiercely contested, mail was important but it was not the Army's first priority. There were four letters from Mama Essie, a letter and a package from Mrs. Merrill. Jeff read Mama Essie's letters first. The letter with the latest date voiced her concerns about the recent Battle of the Bulge, and she cautioned Jeff to be careful. "Son," she wrote, "you tell that general that no matter how much honor they give you, I would rather have you home without honor and alive, than the other way around." Jeff knew that Mama Essie was referring to the statement the general at Fort Wadsworth had made when he was trying to persuade her to allow him to remain in the Army.

Mama Essie did not yet know that he was now an officer. Jeff had written her a letter with the news several days ago, but she had not yet received it. He tried to imagine what her reaction would be when she read his letter.

Next, Jeff read the letter from Mrs. Merrill. Her news kept him abreast of the things that were going on in and around New York and, as always, she cautioned him to be safe and to be positive in his outlook. In the last paragraph she wrote, "It may not be too early to start thinking about what you want to do when you come home." In the package were two catalogues, one from the City

College of New York and the other from Saint John's University. Her letter made no mention of the catalogues. This was typical of Mrs. Merrill. It was her subtle way of getting you to think.

Jeff's pulse quickened at the sight of these books. Mrs. Merrill had spent months helping him to understand ideas and issues he had never heard about, things that were never a conscious part of his world in Alabama. Now she was trying to tell him, in a subtle way, that it was time for him to start thinking about continuing his learning, time to start thinking about a college education. Were her expectations for him too high or had he underestimated himself? He honestly did not know. What he did know was that he had never had the opportunity to earn a high school diploma. He had never even attended high school. Jeff's situation was not unlike that of thousands, perhaps millions, of other black children— children who had been born into abject poverty, the offspring of sharecroppers, children who had only attended school in their spare time. Spare time came only when there was no cotton to pick, no peanuts or corn to be harvested, no fields to be plowed—spare time that left little time for an education.

After leaving the farm, Jeff worked at odd jobs. He had been a delivery boy at several drug stores and he had done yard maintenance at the homes of wealthy white families. Times were difficult. Work for adult black men was hard to find; black children routinely worked to help their families survive. At times, Jeff had attended school, but seldom had he been able to do so on a regular basis. Mama Essie, and Grandma Dawson had taught him and his siblings to read from the Bible. The more he read, the stronger his desire to read grew. Buying books was out of the question. The library was not open to him. There were times when he had been able to salvage old newspapers from the garbage of some of the families who hired him to clean their yards. Until he walked into the library on Staten Island, he had great difficulty in satisfying his strong desire to read more and to read better.

How ironic that today, in what seemed like almost a world away from his roots in Alabama, Jeff was holding in his hands two college catalogues, a strong but subtle hint from Mrs. Merrill—a librarian, his tutor and his strongest advocate—that he needed to think about moving on, to think about preparing himself to enter college. If she had suggested that he try and enter high school, that would have seemed achievable—but college, the very idea was more than he could imagine.

In early 1946, Jeff received his orders to go home. His life in the military had come full circle. It had been a military life that had seen a lot of fighting. He had fought before the JAG and the board of officers at Fort Wadsworth to remain in the Army. With the help of the general and a sympathetic board, he had won that battle. He had fought to stay alive in France and he, along with millions of others, had won that battle as well. Now he was going home, home to Alabama, the place of his greatest heartaches.

Before he could leave this place, there were many things to be done. The most heart-wrenching task was the transfer of his company to a new commander. He had to say his farewell to the noncommissioned officers and the one hundred and eighty men who had embarked upon this journey with him, men who had supported him passionately every step of the way.

The battalion commander had informed Jeff that he had recommended his promotion to first lieutenant, but he was uncertain that the promotion would come through before Jeff left for home. One week before Jeff's scheduled departure, the new company commander was assigned. He was a forty-one-year-old captain whose home was in the state of Maine. At a meeting in his office, the battalion commander introduced Jeff to the captain. In his very blunt remarks, the battalion commander told the captain that he was inheriting the best company in the battalion. He said that the company was accustomed to tough leadership, but that leadership had to be fair and it had to be impartial. He went on to say that these men had, for the first time ever, been privileged to serve under a black commanding officer and it would be difficult for many of them to make the transition back to the status quo. The colonel concluded by saying, "Fairness and good strong leadership will be the decisive factors when you assume command tomorrow."

As Jeff and the new unit commander were about to leave his office, the colonel reached into his desk drawer and presented Jeff with a single silver bar. Jeff had been promoted to first lieutenant. The colonel had a solemn look on his face, one Jeff had seen on past occasions when the colonel wanted to project an air of seriousness. He looked Jeff squarely in the eyes, and he said, "I'm going to miss you greatly, you lucky bastard."

On Jeff's last day of command, First Sergeant Anderson assembled the company in the courtyard. It was a lovely summer day, but a mood of sadness was in the air. Jeff was sad to be leaving so many people he had gone through hell with, people he loved very much. The men were sad for much the same reason, but added to all of this was the simple fact that they were losing a leader they called their own.

Before Jeff and the new company commander came out of the building, First Sergeant Anderson and the platoon sergeants assembled the men in company formation. As Jeff approached the company, First Sergeant Anderson brought them to attention. As they stood at rigid attention, Jeff approached the company and faced the men.

"First Sergeant Anderson reporting, sir. The company is formed."

"Take your post, First Sergeant," Jeff commanded. As the sergeant began to about-face, his eyes gleamed. Jeff had wondered how he was going to control his own emotions in his last official appearance before these men. He now saw First Sergeant Anderson, this hardened combat veteran, having great difficulty holding back his tears.

"Gentlemen," Jeff began, "I have the happy task of presenting to you your new company commander. Captain James Weller will be out in just a few minutes. Now, men," Jeff continued, "I have the sad, very sad task of making my last appearance before you. I will be leaving here tomorrow morning. I want you to know that I appreciate your service to your country, to your battalion, to your company and to me. Wherever I go and whatever I do, the memories of you will always be in my heart. Thank you and may

God bless and keep you just as he has during this long and difficult campaign."

Jeff knew that he would have to end here. His emotions would permit him to go no further. Captain Weller was standing just to the rear of the company and he sensed the difficulty Jeff was having. He marched to a spot directly behind Jeff and took his position. Jeff made an about-face, saluted the captain, and said, "Sir, the company is present and accounted for."

Captain Weller returned Jeff's salute and he said, "Sir, you are dismissed and the prayers and the blessings of all of these men and their new commanding officer go with you."

Captain Weller then commanded First Sergeant Anderson to take his post in front of him. Before Anderson could salute, the captain issued his first order to the men. "First Sergeant," he said, "duty for these men is suspended for the remainder of the day."

The company broke its formation and each man raced for the mess hall. First Sergeant Anderson approached Jeff and said, "Sir, would you consider coming into the mess hall and having a last cup of coffee with us?"

"I would not miss the chance, First Sergeant," Jeff said.

"Give us fifteen to twenty minutes and the senior platoon sergeant will come to your quarters to escort you to the mess hall."

Jeff waited for more than half an hour. He was about to fall asleep on his bed when the senior platoon sergeant knocked on his door. The short walk to the mess hall was made without words being exchanged between the two men. As they entered the hall, the battalion commander, a full colonel, called the men to attention. Jeff was confused. Never in his military career had he seen or heard of a senior officer calling attention for a junior officer, but it had happened here and before his very teary eyes. How was he supposed to react, Jeff wondered. Could he give the "at ease" command with this high-ranking senior officer in the room? The colonel looked at Jeff and nodded his approval. "As you were, men. Be seated," he said.

The colonel had brought with him, the battalion executive officer and the adjutant. The colonel spoke to the men in a loud staccato voice.

"Men," he said, "I'm not going to hang around and spoil your party. I know that you want to celebrate and honor your former commanding officer. I know you want to raise a little hell and you've earned the right to do so. From your rank has come one of the finest officers I have ever been privileged to command. He's not just one of you. Lieutenant Wiggins is one of us all. One last word, it is against Army policy to drink on post, except in designated areas. And the first sergeant has assured me that all those bottles you are hiding in the storage room contain some form of soft drinks. Is he correct?"

"Yes, sir," was the loud, collective reply.

"That's fine," the colonel said. "Again, Lieutenant, we wish you good luck and when you sail into New York harbor, be sure to salute the Statue of Liberty."

The first sergeant called attention, Jeff saluted the colonel and he and his officers departed. Before the door could close behind the colonel and his party, there was a beehive of activity. Within minutes, bottles of every description appeared from every corner of the room—French cognac, wines, calvados and beer from the United States and Great Britain. First Sergeant Anderson and the platoon sergeant popped several bottles of champagne and the squad leaders poured it into the canteen cups of each man. First Sergeant Anderson tapped his canteen cup and the room immediately fell silent.

"Men," the sergeant began, "we always knew this day was bound to come, but we had hoped that it would come at a later time. Our leader is leaving us and we're sad to see him go. I hope you'll join me in a toast to wish this young company commander 'Godspeed', wherever life takes him."

He then turned to Jeff and said, "Lieutenant, it has been our pleasure, correction, it has been our privilege to serve with you. There were times when you were very tough on us; you had to be. But there was never a time when you failed to be fair. None of us here ever dreamed that we would have the opportunity to serve under a black commander, but we have. Our spirits have been lifted and, through your actions and leadership, you have shown us all that if we have a vision for ourselves, and if we're willing to pay the price, we can achieve the things embodied in that vision. We'll miss you, sir, and we'll never forget you."

First Sergeant Anderson, along with the rest of the company, raised his canteen cup in a final salute to Jeff. Sergeant Anderson downed the contents of his cup in what seemed to Jeff like one giant gulp and he turned and walked briskly out of the room. Emotions were running high and Jeff wished that he, too, could leave. But he could not leave before shaking hands with and saying goodbye to each man in the room.

CHAPTER TWENTY-FOUR

On the seven days he spent aboard the troop ship headed for New York, Jeff had time to reflect and to collect his thoughts in a way that had not been possible over the past three and a half years. Did he really want to leave the Army, or did he want to try to become a career soldier? These were questions that cried out for an answer, but he knew that he was neither emotionally nor intellectually prepared to answer at this time.

He was a first lieutenant in the United States Army, he was black and he had absolutely no experience as an adult in the civilian world. How would all of this factor into his decision? If he left the Army and went back into civilian life, was he prepared to accept the life of humiliation, segregation and exclusion that he had run away from just a few years ago? This question he could answer now and without hesitation. The answer was an emphatic "No". In the Army, he had been judged on merit and he had advanced up the ranks based upon his ability and performance. Jeff easily concluded that he could not settle for a life that offered him anything less than the same kind of opportunity.

In his bags aboard the ship were the catalogues that Mrs. Merrill had sent to him. Maybe he should take a closer look at them, but why? He didn't have a high school diploma. Surely, no college was going to admit him without it. In reality, there was no guarantee that he could or would be admitted to college even if he did have a diploma. Jeff had never set foot on a college campus; he had never even seen a college. He had no concept of what college was like or whether or not he would be college material. He had sixty days to make a decision about leaving or remaining in the Army and he planned to use that time wisely to decide what direction his future would take.

The ship docked at a pier in Manhattan, but as it first sailed into New York harbor, Jeff kept his promise to the battalion commander. He saluted the Statue of Liberty. Somehow this salute seemed right and proper. Jeff had that surge of pride that forms when you feel that you have successfully completed a difficult task.

Upon his arrival in Manhattan, Jeff was immediately sent to Fort Drum in upstate New York and was given a sixty-day leave. He returned to Manhattan, checked in at the Hotel Theresa in Harlem and saw a few sights before taking the ferry to Staten Island to visit Mrs. Merrill at the library. He was nervous and apprehensive about seeing her again. Would she know him? So much had changed since he had last seen her. He was almost three years older, three inches taller, and thirty-five pounds heavier. The olive drab uniform and the stripes he wore as a sergeant had been replaced with the pink and green uniform of a commissioned officer. The stripes on his arms had been replaced with a silver bar on each shoulder, denoting the rank of first lieutenant. Would Mrs. Merrill recognize him in the light of these changes? Would his own mother, Mama Essie, recognize him?

The south ferry to Staten Island seemed very familiar. He had made the trip from Staten Island to Manhattan many times during his tour of duty at Fort Wadsworth. But this trip was different from any other trip he had taken. Soldiers in large numbers were still present in New York. On the ferry, Jeff noticed a group of more than a dozen enlisted men who were staring intently at him. Among the group were two black soldiers. Jeff moved from his seat inside the ferry to a place on the deck. He was trying to imagine his reunion with Mrs. Merrill after an absence of almost three years. He looked around from his position on the deck. Standing near him was the same group of soldiers who had been staring so intently at him inside the ferry. Finally, one of the black soldiers slowly approached him, nervously saluted and said, "Good afternoon, sir."

"Good afternoon, soldier," Jeff replied.

"I hope you don't mind us looking at you, sir."

Jeff interrupted the soldier and asked, "Haven't you ever seen an officer before now?"

"Yes, sir," the soldier replied, "but we've never seen a black officer before. Sir," the soldier said as he awkwardly held his camera, "would it be possible to have my picture taken with you?"

"It would be my pleasure," Jeff replied. The soldier beckoned his buddies to come over, and for the next few minutes, Jeff posed for pictures with each of the soldiers.

The soldier saluted Jeff before leaving. "Just wait until my mother sees me in a picture with an officer," he beamed.

The second black soldier said, "Not just an officer, a black officer!"

Upon his arrival at the Staten Island library, Jeff paid the white taxi cab driver. As he was leaving the cab, the driver shouted, "Hey, man. I've never seen anybody like you wearing an officer's uniform." It was at this point, more than at anytime in the past, that Jeff realized that wherever he went in this uniform, many eyes would be gazing at him.

When he entered the library he did not immediately see Mrs. Merrill. He walked over to the card catalog and asked another librarian if Mrs. Merrill was in. The librarian looked around to see if she could locate Mrs. Merrill, but before she could respond, Jeff felt a light tap on his shoulder. He turned, and came face to face with the woman who had played such a vital role in his life. After a very emotional embrace, she said, "How do I address you? Do I call you 'General'?"

Jeff smiled at Mrs. Merrill and said, "You never speak to a general unless he speaks to you first."

They exchanged a few more words and she said, "This calls for a real celebration."

"I agree," Jeff said. Mrs. Merrill engaged in a brief conversation with one of her colleagues, came to the table where Jeff was sitting and announced that she was taking the rest of the day off. They went to a small Italian restaurant on Staten Island where everyone seemed to know her. Mrs. Merrill ordered a glass of wine. She said Jeff should get a soft drink.

The waiter, who was also the owner, seemed puzzled. "Soldiers," he said, "have soft drinks when there's nothing else available. I have all kinds of booze in this joint," he said. "What would you like, Lieutenant?"

"Bourbon and soda will be fine," Jeff answered.

"Sal," Mrs. Merrill protested, "the lieutenant is too young to be drinking hard liquor."

"Anna Marie," Sal replied, "when someone shoots at you and you shoot back, you are no longer 'young', no matter what your age."

Over dinner, Jeff brought Mrs. Merrill up to date on the events he could not tell her about in letters. She wanted to know every detail. When he had exhausted his memory, she said, "Lieutenant, now what?"

"I don't really know. I have a lot to think about," Jeff answered. She looked intently into Jeff's eyes. Her own blue eyes seemed filled with the excitement he had seen in her many times before.

"Young man," she said, "there is only one thing you should be thinking about and that one thing is the furtherance of your education. You must enroll in a good college."

Jeff became a bit irritated and she sensed it. He was irritated partly because she seemed able to look into his soul and see things that he would be content to ignore.

"I received the college catalogues you sent me and I read them thoroughly. But how do you propose that I get into college? I barely got out of grammar school and I don't have a high school diploma. Is it realistic for you or me to think that any college will admit me?"

"Jeff, you listen to me and focus on every word I say. Realism is what we make it. I repeat, realism is what we make it."

The decibel of her voice had risen to the point where Sal came over to the table and inquired if everything was all right. She snapped at Sal. "I may have to hit this young man over the head with this booth, but otherwise everything is fine!"

Sal retreated to his position behind the counter, but before he left, he turned to Jeff and said, "Lieutenant, whatever the fight is about, surrender. This is one battle you can't win."

Mrs. Merrill's eyes remained focused on Jeff. "A few short years ago," she continued, "a confused, teenage farm boy walked into a

New York library, desperately seeking to better his lot. He listened, he studied, he stayed focused and he was a fast learner. That young soldier, that boy-man, went off to war and somewhere out there somebody recognized that he was special, that he had the innate ability to lead men and he did. Now the man who was that boy— a first lieutenant in the United States Army—is sitting here trying to prove to me that he does not have what it takes to get into college. Did the Germans make a way for you and all of the other men to get on to Normandy beach? No, they did not. You made your own way. You made it happen. It was a battle you knew you could not afford to lose. You fought like hell, because it was hell, and you won. Lieutenant," she said, "this is a battle, too. The battle for a good college education is a battle you and I cannot afford to lose."

Her face was flushed, and her blue eyes seemed to be on fire. She was trying to motivate him and she was succeeding.

"I'll send a petition to the Board of Education in your hometown. I'll outline your accomplishments and ask them to award you a high school diploma based upon your achievements. If and when a diploma is awarded, we will proceed from there. But one way or the other, you will be enrolled in some college, somewhere in this country. Your government has placed a law on the books that guarantees you the opportunity to go to a school of your choice. This law is called the G.I. Bill of Rights. The money to pay for your education is in the bank. This may be the best opportunity you'll ever have to help yourself, to secure your future. I won't allow you to squander it."

Jeff just gazed into the eyes of this woman who was so adamant in her position. He was still amazed at her advocacy on his behalf. He was trying, through the sheer force of will, to capture some of the confidence she had in him, to force her confidence to engulf and energize him. Mrs. Merrill was almost reading his mind, he thought. Before he could respond to the things she had said, she took a deep breath, lowered her voice and spoke more softly.

"Jeff, if you don't further your education, what is the alternative? As I see it, you can remain in the Army, or you can return to

Alabama. If you decide to remain in the Army, your service will be on an almost day-to-day basis. It's only a question of a very short time before all of the branches of the armed services will require their officers to have a college degree. The weapons of war will become increasingly more sophisticated, requiring more highly trained personnel. The service chiefs will select officers from an elite group of college graduates. If you return to Alabama, you'll probably be returning to a slightly modified form of the life you ran away from just a few years ago. The Klan may not burn a cross on your front lawn, because they, too, are refining their ways. But they are still just as resolute in their intentions. Instead of hanging you from a tree, they now strangle you with humiliation and they lynch you economically. No matter how they do it, you're dead. Physically or psychologically you will slowly die. Is this what you fought for?"

Jeff knew better than to interrupt Mrs. Merrill. Sal was right. This was a battle he had no hope of winning. He sat before her, listening intently.

Finally she said, "Do you recall the last talk we had before you left for Fort Leonard Wood, and then for Europe?"

"I don't recall specifically," Jeff answered. "We probably discussed many things."

"Well, let me remind you, Lieutenant Jeff. You asked me how you could ever pay me for all of the help I tried to give to you—the nightly hours of tutoring, trying to enhance you intellectually, trying to build your confidence and self-esteem, to bolster your sense of self-worth. Do you remember?"

"I remember clearly," Jeff nodded. "How can I ever forget what you did and continue to do for me?"

"All right young man, I want to be paid. You owe me, and I demand payment. I don't need money. I am not talking about money. You can pay me," she said, "by resolving to pursue a college education with the same zeal, the same focus, you used to further your military career. I will consider anything less than this as a default. I want for you the things I would want for my own son, if I had a son," she ended.

Jeff started to speak but she said, "No more talk today. Enough has been said. Sal, bring me the check," she demanded.

"The lieutenant has already paid the bill," Sal said. He looked at Jeff and placed his finger on his lips.

On the ferry ride back to Manhattan, Jeff was in deep thought about what Mrs. Merrill had said. He did owe her; there was absolutely no doubt about that. He began to recall the first time he had met her. He had been very nervous about walking into this building called a "library". During his childhood in Alabama, he had often passed the red and white, very large brick building that housed the library. He had never attempted to enter that building. It was absolutely forbidden for any black person to enter. He had no idea what he was looking for or what he would see when he entered that Staten Island library. What he had encountered was an amazing world of books, magazines, periodicals and much more. Now, sitting here on the ferry, he could imagine how he must have looked and sounded on that day. He had not expected help from this lady, nor from anyone else for that matter, but there she stood— tall, kindly and elegant—asking him what he was looking for and how could she help him find it. It was a reversal of what he had known in Alabama. There, under the law, people he knew found ways to keep him out of the library. On Staten Island, a stranger, a nameless woman had offered her help. "Whatever it is that you're looking for, I may be able to help you find it," she had said. The problem was, he had no clue as to what he was looking for. Jeff almost laughed out loud as he thought of how dumb and unsophisticated he must have appeared to her that day. After looking back over all of these events, Jeff had long ago decided that Mrs. Merrill was far from being an ordinary woman.

As the ferry docked at South Street, he scrambled for a train to 125th Street and his hotel. On the train, he tried to dissect, to examine Mrs. Merrill's motives. Why had she taken an interest in him? What was it that had propelled him into the presence of this person? He had nothing to offer to her except his ignorance, his lack of knowledge. What was she looking to find in him?

As the train made its stop at Times Square, Jeff could not dismiss a nagging thought, a sensation that he could not dismiss. It almost seemed that Mama Essie was sitting beside him, trying to tell him something he should know. She was trying to answer a question he had asked when he was seven, maybe eight years old. He could now recall the day, probably a Sunday, when Mama Essie had summoned him and his siblings to read passages from the Bible. Jeff had read a passage from the Book of Revelations. In that passage, he had read about an angel flying in mid-heaven, proclaiming that he had everlasting good news. Try as he may, he could not recall the chapter or verse from which he was reading, but he could recall asking Mama Essie if there were angels on earth. Her reply had been prompt and emphatic.

"God's angels," she said, "are all over the earth."

"Why can't I find one?" he remembered asking.

"Son," she replied, "you don't have to find an angel. When the time is right, the angel will find you."

Had the time been right on the day he walked into the Staten Island library? Had an angel who called herself "Anna Marie Merrill" found him? These questions plagued him so much that he lost track of time and the station where he was supposed to exit. When Jeff finally looked up, he was two stops past where he should have been.

Jeff had great difficulty sleeping that night. Mrs. Merrill's words kept ringing in his ears. "You owe me and I want to be paid," she had said. The next morning, over a leisurely breakfast in the hotel dining room, Jeff determined that he would call Mrs. Merrill and ask her how he could settle his debt with her. At midmorning, he placed a call to the library. She came to the phone with a pleasant, upbeat voice.

"How did you sleep last night?" she asked

"Not very well," Jeff answered.

"That's fine," she said. "I hope you used the sleepless time to think about what we discussed."

"I spend a sleepless night and you think that's fine?" Jeff said to her.

"What caused you the most sleepless moments?"

"The statement about 'owing you and paying you'," Jeff said. "I know how much I owe. But what bothers me more than anything else is how I pay you. If you'll just tell me how, I can start to feel a little better about myself."

"Stop!" she shouted into the phone. "You may be very bright about military things, but you seem mighty naive about the things that matter most. What I'm talking about is your future and the future of all of the people you will touch and who will touch you. In the war that just concluded, you lived from day to day. You had no time or desire to think much about the future because you knew that your future could very well be the next bullet, artillery blast or mortar shell. That's all in your past now and, like it or not, you must begin to look ahead. Again I say, you owe me and you can only pay me by paying yourself. You can pay yourself by doing everything that's in your power to assure yourself and me that you'll have a future that is unlike your past.

"Alabama isn't the place for you at this time in your life. It may be in years to come, but not now. Neither you, nor your family nor anyone else can fight and defeat the Ku Klux Klan with the guns you depended on so much in Europe. The Klan knows all about guns and ropes. They used them to acquire whatever power they believe they have. The only means by which you can achieve an overwhelming victory over these bigots, and all other bigots for that matter, is through education. Expose them through knowledge. I insist, no, I demand that you get your high school diploma and go on to college where you'll acquire that knowledge. When you have done these two things, Lieutenant Jeff, you will have paid yourself and you will have paid me. The slate will be clean; you will then be free.

"I hope you will always remember that freedom carries with it great responsibilities. When you free yourself it obligates you to look around and help to free others who are looking to share in what you have. They, too, need help. It's your responsibility to provide that help wherever you can."

Jeff was badly shaken by what Mrs. Merrill had said over the phone. He was pleased that their conversation had not taken place face to face. He certainly would not have wanted her to see his emotional reaction to what she had said. She was right. Jeff knew deep within his soul that she was right and he made a vow that he would pay himself and, in doing so, he would pay her.

They met later that night. Mrs. Merrill wanted to meet at the library. She said she had matters to finalize with him before he left New York to visit his family in Alabama. Seated in Mrs. Merrill's small office, Jeff watched as she prepared a letter to the Board of Education in his hometown. Her letter requested that he be awarded a high school diploma based upon his experiences, his military achievements, and his work with her over the years. Jeff had tentatively decided that if he was awarded the high school diploma, he would like to gain admission to a college in Tennessee. So Mrs. Merrill prepared a letter for the Admissions Officer at Tennessee State University in Nashville.

On the train headed for his home in Alabama, Jeff had time to think about what it would be like to again be in a place he called "home", but in a social atmosphere for which he had complete contempt. Would they now see him as a "boy" like they had always seen his father and all other black men? Or would they at least pay some respect to the uniform he wore? It did not take long for him to see just how little things had changed.

When the train arrived in Washington, D.C., the laws of the North gave way to the laws of the South and those Southern laws clearly forbid the integration of the races under any circumstances. The front cars of the train nearest to the engine were reserved for "colored"; all other cars were for "whites only". It seemed such a contradiction to Jeff. He and hundreds of thousands of soldiers of his race could fight to help liberate a white Europe, only to return home to find that the liberty they had helped to return to Europe was not available to them in the very place they called "home".

As the train sped through Virginia and the Carolinas, Mrs. Merrill's words kept ringing in his ears. "When you have done these two things," she had said, "then you will have paid me and the slate will be clean. You will be free."

If Jeff needed a demonstration of how prophetic her words

were, he needed to look no further than this rigidly segregated train. He was determined now, more than at any time in the recent past, to pay her, to pay himself and to obtain his freedom. One way or another, he would get that high school diploma and he would go on to whatever college would admit him. Whatever was required, he would do it.

Jeff fell asleep. The thoughts running through his mind had left him exhausted. The conductor tapping his shoulder awakened him.

"Lieutenant," he announced, "Get ready, yours is the next stop. Ten minutes."

His heartbeat quickened, he had not seen Mama Essie and the rest of his family in more than three years. She would be waiting at the small railroad station. He knew that it would be an emotional reunion. He also knew that she had worried about him during the entire course of the war. She was relieved when the conflict ended. His letters had kept her informed of how he was doing but military censorship prevented him from telling her much about what he was doing.

When the train came to a stop, he saw a large crowd. Some people were waiting for arrivals, others were waiting to board the train. Mama Essie saw him before he could find her in the large crowd. Just as he had predicted, it was an extremely emotional reunion. It was midday and there were several black men and women onlookers. All eyes were on Jeff as he attempted to get through the crowd with his large bag. He and Mama Essie attempted to struggle toward the taxicab stand, but the going was slow. There were half a dozen black soldiers exiting the train; two came over to Jeff, after pushing their way through the crowd. They grabbed his bag and said, "Sir, may we help you?" One summoned a taxi and opened the cab door to let Jeff and Mama Essie get into the cab. Before the cab pulled way from the curb, one of the soldiers stood at rigid attention, saluted, and said, "Sir, you are the first one of us we have ever seen."

At home, Mama Essie was very parochial. She wanted Jeff alone. She wanted him to herself for a while. The last time they had seen each other was in the JAG's office at Fort Wadsworth. That was almost three years ago. She had, at that time, said goodbye to her little boy. Now, she was attempting to become reacquainted with a man who was, in his mother's eyes, still her little boy.

During the three weeks he remained at home, he was barely able to get out of Mama Essie's sight. She brought Jeff up to date on all family matters. Mama Essie was doing well financially. Most of Jeff's Army pay went to her. After he had been home for a week, Jeff asked his mother about his father. She told him that his father had moved back to Alabama and was living across town. Jeff went to the address his mother had given him but his father wasn't at home. A neighbor told him that he could find his father at the restaurant down the street.

Upon entering the restaurant, Jeff immediately recognized his father sitting in a booth. As he approached the booth, it was obvious that his father didn't have a clue as to who he was. Jeff took a seat in the booth.

"I haven't seen the likes of you around here," the man scoffed.

Jeff smiled as his father continued to talk. "I have a boy in the Army," he said. "My boy's a first lieutenant and I expect that he'll be home almost any day now. My boy," he went on, "was a company commander during the Battle of the Bulge. He's a highly decorated soldier and he takes no shit from anyone!"

Jeff laughed out loud and he could tell that this irritated his father. "Old man," Jeff said, "I don't believe you have a son and even if you do have a son, he can't be all of the things you say he is."

His father's eyes flashed with anger and his body stiffened. Jeff continued, "If by some chance what you say is true, I don't believe you'd even recognize your so-called son if he stared you in the eyes."

His father rose from the booth and Jeff was certain that his father was about to strike him. Instead, his father spoke. "You disrespectful bastard. You come in here, you sit in my booth, at my table, and you tell me that I have no son and that I wouldn't recognize my son if I saw him. Before I reach into my waistband

and get my gun and blow your miserable brains out, I'm going to give you a chance to leave. Now get the hell out of my sight, you ugly son of a bitch you."

This meeting was getting out of hand quickly. Jeff reached into his pocket and took out his Army identification card that had his picture attached to it. This action on Jeff's part just seemed to make matters worse. Jeff had forgotten for a moment that his father was totally illiterate. He could not read. Jeff spoke softly. "Daddy, I'm your boy. I'm Jeff." But his father was so overcome with anger that he was not listening to anything Jeff said. Mr. Gus, the restaurant owner, and a longtime friend of the family, stepped forward. "Clem, calm yourself. This is your son. This is First Lieutenant Jeff. He was just testing your memory and your sense of humor."

A broad smile crossed Clem's face. "I knew it all along," he said, "I just wanted to have a little fun with the boy."

From that point forward, things changed. What had been an air of confrontation became jovial and family like. Jeff's father invited everyone in the restaurant over to meet his son. He told anyone who would listen, "My son is a personal friend of General Patton's". Jeff whispered to his father that he was not General Patton's friend.

"I met him for only a few fleeting minutes, Daddy. Lowly lieutenants are never friends of generals. They serve under the general's command, but this doesn't qualify as friendship."

"You knew him, didn't you?"

"Yes, Daddy, but he didn't know me, except for about four or five minutes."

Jeff knew that his father was embarrassed about his inability to recognize his own son when they first met. His father did all that he could to make up for this by staying as close to Jeff as possible. Each morning before Jeff was out of bed, his father came to Mama Essie's house and sat on the front porch, waiting for his son to appear. He never knocked on the door or gave any signal that he was there. He just sat and waited.

CHAPTER TWENTY-FIVE

During the three weeks that Jeff was in Alabama, he and Mama Essie spoke about many things. Jeff was especially interested in her financial well-being. He wanted her to be comfortable. She had been able to afford so little for so much of her life. Mama Essie assured him that the she was doing well. In the past three years, she had been able to move into a decent house, buy the clothing she needed and maintain a healthy diet. Mama Essie said that a few years ago it would have been hard for her to visualize that she would be in such a comfortable position. Her life up to that point had been one of constant struggle, for herself and for her children.

Jeff brought Mama Essie up to date about the things Mrs. Merrill wanted him to do. "Bless that woman," Mama Essie said, "but I just don't think that the Board of Education will give you a diploma. They should, but I'm afraid they'll only see you as 'uppity' when they find out what you've done. The war changed a few things around here," she continued, "but feelings about race haven't changed."

Jeff called Mrs. Merrill at the end of his second week at home. She told him that she had sent a registered letter to the superintendent of schools in his hometown requesting that he be awarded a diploma based upon his military experience and achievements. Supporting documents such as letters from his former company commander and the JAG as well as a copy of the proclamation signed by President Harry Truman authorizing his commission as an officer in the United States Army, accompanied her letter. Mrs. Merrill was upbeat. She said that she expected a quick, positive reply.

At the end of his three-week stay in Alabama, Jeff returned to New York. He still had thirty days remaining on his sixty-day leave. He and Mrs. Merrill agreed that it would be best for him to be in New York. There would be college applications to be completed after he received his diploma.

For the next month, Jeff took up residence on West 155th Street with his adopted Aunt Lila. Jeff suspected that Mrs. Merrill wanted him out of Alabama and in New York because she feared that, in Alabama, a state of complacency would seize him and his zest for continuing his education would be diminished. Mrs. Merrill scheduled meetings with him three times each week. They held drills that sharpened his English and math skills. They talked extensively about what he could expect in a college environment and, on two occasions, they visited college campuses—New York University and Fordham University.

At the end of his month's stay in New York, there was still no reply from the Board of Education in Alabama. Mrs. Merrill was deeply disturbed that there had been no word, not even a rejection. It was now two days before Jeff was scheduled to return to Fort Drum for his final separation from the Army. It worried them that Jeff would be separated from the Army without having college as an alternative. Without a diploma from high school, his chances of being admitted to any college were zero.

In a desperate effort to get a response from the Board of Education, Mrs. Merrill placed a long-distance call to the superintendent of schools and to the chairwoman of the Board of Education. The chairwoman assured her that the matter would be taken up by the full board at their next regularly scheduled meeting that would be held in two weeks.

Jeff returned to Fort Drum and was able to get his discharge date extended for another sixty days, but at the end of this two-month period, his separation from the Army would be final. He returned to New York and again took up residence with Aunt Lila.

Three weeks later, Mrs. Merrill received a letter from the Board of Education in Alabama. The letter advised that it would be necessary for Jeff to appear personally before the full board in order for the board to give any consideration to her request.

"At least they didn't say 'no'," she stated. "Will you go back to Alabama and appear before them?"

"I'll go," Jeff said. "And I'll appear before the board in full dress uniform."

Jeff continued to see Mrs. Merrill three times each week. She tried to anticipate some of the questions the board might ask. Mrs. Merrill fashioned a number of questions, some friendly, others hostile. "No matter what they ask you," she said, "you must maintain an air of civility. You can disarm them with your composure and your dignity."

Jeff arrived back in Alabama three days before his scheduled appearance before the board. Mama Essie was happy that the board was giving him the opportunity to make his case, but she had serious doubts that the outcome would be positive. Jeff's attitude was upbeat. He sincerely believed that if the board allowed him to completely explain what forces converged to lead him here, the outcome would be favorable. He had obtained as much information as he could get about the background of each board member. For the most part, the board members were prominent local businessmen and women. He was sure that they would ask hard questions, but most were seen as fair-minded people. However, Jeff was told that there were three members who would probably not be inclined to render a vote that would be favorable to him. These three members stood between him and a high school diploma. These three people threatened his future.

When he was finally called into the large room, there were, perhaps, one hundred or more spectators seated there. The chairwoman of the board spoke first. "Please have a seat, Lieutenant," she said. "You are appearing before us with an unusual request. You are demanding that this board award you a high school diploma simply because you spent time in the Army. Is this correct?"

What a loaded question, Jeff thought. If this question was designed to set the tone of the meeting, he certainly could not afford to answer in the way he believed the chairwoman anticipated. Somehow he had to extinguish these embers before they burst into full flame. The room was deathly quiet as the chairwoman waited for his response.

"I can certainly agree with the chairwoman," Jeff began, "that my request for a diploma is unusual. But I respectfully request that the word 'demand' be stricken, and that it be replaced with the word, 'request'. I make no demands for anything that is not rightfully mine. Again, ma'am, I request that you consider awarding me a diploma based upon the facts and documents before you."

"Wouldn't it have been easier for you to have remained at home and gotten your diploma the same way as every other boy and girl?"

"Yes, ma'am, it would have been easier if other things had been equal, but other things were not equal. That's why I'm here tonight."

"Other things," the chairwoman said, "seemed to be equal for you in the United States Army, would you concede me that?"

"I would concede, ma'am, that they were more equal," Jeff stated.

The questioning was taken over by another member of the board, a gentleman farmer, who owned and farmed thousands of acres throughout the county. "Lieutenant," he began, "you're still young enough to enroll in school and get your diploma a more conventional way."

Jeff sat looking directly at the man.

"Are you going to answer my question?"

"What was your question, sir?" Jeff asked.

"Don't play games with me, boy," he said.

"I would not presume to play games with you, sir. I thought you were making a statement." Jeff tried to keep the tone of his voice even and respectful. He saw that this man was trying to incite him to say the wrong thing. He would not respond to the word "boy".

At this point, another member of the board, a woman, pulled a microphone closer to her and shouted, "Madam Chairwoman, I must interrupt here, to protest the line and the tone of the questions. We seem to be heaping upon this young man, this United States Army officer, insults that he does not deserve. There is no law that requires us to award him a diploma, but common courtesy ought to dictate that we treat him with the dignity and respect I believe he deserves. He is not a 'boy'. He's an officer, a first lieutenant, sitting here before us in full dress uniform. If this line of questioning continues, I'll leave this meeting."

Jeff breathed a sigh of relief. This woman, a member of the board, had said all of the things he dared not say. A heated discussion broke out between members of the board. The chairwoman banged her gavel and stated that the board would be adjourned for twenty minutes.

When the board members left the room, Jeff and Mama Essie went out into the hallway to wait for the meeting to resume. An older man, his wife and son approached them. The son asked Jeff if he could explain to his father the meaning of each of the medals he wore. Jeff began, but the son said, "Lieutenant, would you mind if I explained?"

"Not at all," Jeff said. The son began to meticulously name the medals and explain why Jeff wore them. Ten medals were described. The young man turned to Mama Essie and inquired, "Is this your son?"

"Yes, he's my son," she replied.

"Well," said the young man, "I don't like the way things are going here and I'm going to speak my mind when the board comes back into session. Do you agree?" He addressed his remarks to Mama Essie.

"I do agree," she said. "But you could make matters worse if you speak out."

"Worse?" he said. "Things can't get much worse than they are now. Somebody has to have the guts to speak out, and dammit, I'm gonna do it," the young man said.

The board returned to the hearing room and was again in session. The superintendent took up the questioning at this point. "Lieutenant," he said, "like each member of this board, I appreciate the service you have rendered to your country, but, speaking for myself and only for myself, I just don't see how I can vote to award you a diploma under the circumstance outlined here. If we gave you a diploma, we would have to award a diploma to every Tom,

Dick, and Harry who comes before this board under like circumstances."

At this point, the young man rose to his feet and approached the microphone. For the first time, Jeff noticed that he walked with a slight limp. His face mirrored the faces of many injured soldiers Jeff had seen who tried to hide their real pain.

"Madam Chairlady," he began, "I came to this meeting tonight to speak to you about another matter, but that can wait for another time. The matter the board is discussing now is far more important. I don't know the man whose fate you have in your hands. We met in the hallway about fifteen minutes ago. I don't know him personally, but I know his history. His history in the United States Army is written on his chest. The ten medals he is wearing each tell a separate story. When you put all ten of these stories together, you get a complete and compelling story.

"I served in the military and I fought in the Pacific. I was a Marine and I have a silver plate in my head and a lot of shrapnel in my leg to prove how vicious war can be. I never rose to this officer's rank, but I know that they don't give silver bars on a first come, first serve basis. This lieutenant got his commission the hard way. He got a battle field commission." The young man's voice was at a fever pitch now.

He continued, "The superintendent just said 'every Tom, Dick, and Harry with like circumstances' will come before this board and the board would have to award them a diploma, too. I can assure you, this will not be a problem. There is not another person in this state whose circumstances are like this officer's. Look at him! No, don't do that, because if you look at his face, your decision will be easy. Look at his achievements, his potential, search your souls, and then make a decision. I say to you, ladies and gentlemen, give the lieutenant his diploma. He's earned it and a lot more."

The young man sat down as his father whispered something into his ear and gave him a pat on the back. The room fell silent. No one moved; no one looked around except Jeff and Mama Essie. They both realized that this young man, despite his good intentions and spoken truth, might have actually harmed their cause.

The board chairwoman slammed her gavel down and announced that the board would be in recess for ten minutes. Jeff and Mama Essie walked out into the hallway again. Their thoughts were almost the same—this fair-minded young man had alienated the members of the Board of Education by backing them into a corner. He had clearly intended to help Jeff, but they feared that his words had actually hurt.

The outspoken young man again approached Jeff and Mama Essie. He held out his hand to Jeff and said, "Sir, they'll probably accuse me of being a nigger lover, but I'm not that at all. I'm a lover of fairness and justice." After he finished speaking, he walked out of the building. Jeff noticed that his limp was now more pronounced.

The board returned to the room at the end of about ten minutes. The chairwoman again banged her gavel down and began speaking directly to Jeff.

"Lieutenant," she said, "the board will direct the principal of your local high school to prepare a high school transcript and open a file for you immediately. If, and when you seek to enroll in college, the record will show that you have the proper credentials."

Before Jeff could say "thank you", the gavel came down abruptly and the board members filed out of the room. Mama Essie looked at Jeff. Her eyes were filled with tears but she managed to say, "Son, you have your high school diploma."

The next morning, Jeff called Mrs. Merrill in New York as she had told him to do. He promptly told her that the board had awarded him the diploma. She was in high spirits. "Mister," she said, "get yourself back to New York as soon as possible. I have applications from several colleges. You'll have to select the one that you believe will best fulfill your needs and career goals." She continued, "Just bear in mind that we have lots of work to do if you expect to be admitted in September."

After the talk with Mrs. Merrill, Jeff and Mama Essie spoke at length. Mama Essie said, "Jeff, it seems as if you've lived a lifetime already."

"I couldn't have done all of these things without the support of you and Mrs. Merrill," Jeff said.

Mama Essie replied, "God bless that woman, she was sent by God."

On the train back to New York, Jeff was much more relaxed than he had been on his trip down to Alabama. He knew that Mrs. Merrill would like him to enroll in a New York college, but she continued to say that it had to be an institution that he was comfortable with. In the last several weeks, he had had the opportunity to talk to four or five people who had graduated from Tennessee State University in Nashville, Tennessee. Each of these people gave the university very high ratings and they spoke forcefully about the personal attention the faculty was always willing to give to students who needed their help. Jeff felt that, with his academic background—or lack of it—he might very well be a candidate for help. He also knew that walking onto a college campus as a student was a lot different than running along the beach at Normandy or being in command of a company during the Battle of the Bulge. His whole life was about to take a three-hundred-and-sixty-degree turn. He knew that he was about to face the impact of what he had missed because he had not been able to attend school normally as a child. He was confident that his military training and the self-discipline that it brought into his life would serve him well on the college campus or in any endeavor he undertook. There was no turning back now. In another month, he would be released from active duty in the Army. Going back to Alabama was not an option.

When the train arrived in New York, he deposited his things at Aunt Lila's apartment, got a good night's sleep and called Mrs. Merrill. She was in an unusually good mood and she said that she planned to take the following day off so that Jeff's college applications could be completed. She directed Jeff to meet her at the main library in Manhattan at eleven o'clock.

All day long they sat in the library, discussing the pros and the cons of a New York college with its very large student population versus Tennessee State University, with its smaller student body and its ability to give individual and personal help. By late afternoon the decision was jointly made that Tennessee State would be his first choice.

After the college admissions forms were completed, they turned their attention to the Veteran's Administration. The G.I. Bill of Rights guaranteed that, under certain conditions, veterans were entitled to four years of educational and training benefits. Jeff qualified for four years of college as well as a cash stipend for each month he was enrolled in college and remained in good academic standing.

With all this paperwork completed, the stage was set for his final step toward admission. Before forwarding the completed application to Tennessee State University, Mrs. Merrill placed phone calls to both the director of admissions and the academic dean. She was assured that, if Jeff could pass an admissions test, he would be admitted to the university.

Mrs. Merrill forwarded the application by special delivery. She used her home address for any return communication from the university. The wait to hear when he would have to go to the university for an interview and testing was an anxious time for Jeff. It seemed to him that he was again entering an unknown world. His feelings were very similar to the feelings he had on that morning, four years ago, when he boarded the Greyhound bus for Fort Benning, Georgia. He was now running away from a life that he knew and liked to a life that was so foreign that the thought of it left him nervous and filled with anxiety.

Jeff wanted to wait another thirty days before being formally separated from the Army. He saw this as a safety net in case the university rejected him. Mrs. Merrill disagreed. She urged Jeff to believe in himself and make a clean break from the military. "You have to do this now," she said. "Today is the beginning of a new and exciting second life for you."

Two days after his separation from the Army, the letter from Tennessee State arrived at Mrs. Merrill's home. Jeff had been invited to come to the university during the next two weeks for an interview and testing. Mrs. Merrill was elated with this good news. She called Sal at the little Italian restaurant and made dinner reservations. Jeff tried, as best he could, to be festive and to act happy, but he could feel pangs of doubt. Suppose he failed the entrance exam? How would he stack up against students who came from good academic backgrounds? Would he be able to keep pace? Indeed, was he college material?

Sal spoke to them as they entered the restaurant. His focus was mainly on Jeff. "I'm going to get you a double bourbon," he said. "You look like you just came face to face with the ghost of death. Cheer up, my friend," he continued. "Whatever it is, we can deal with it."

"Leave him alone," Mrs. Merrill chanted. "He'll be all right. Two days from now, he'll be going to Tennessee to formally begin the process of enrolling in college."

The dinner was a long one, with Mrs. Merrill doing most of the talking. "I can understand," she began, "how different this experience will be for you, but you must not overlook or doubt your own ability. The young students you'll encounter have their anxieties, too. None will have had your experience or appreciation for life and death, what it means and how it changes you. Most will not have traveled very far from home. You've been almost half way around the world and you've seen and heard things they, hopefully, will never have to see and hear. You have a quick mind and good listening skills. Stop being doubtful and try being positive. Just tell yourself over and over again, 'I can do it, I can do it' and I promise you that you can do it."

Back at Aunt Lila's late that night, Jeff had difficulty getting to sleep. He was no longer in the United States Army where he felt secure. He was no longer in Alabama where he felt stifled by the rigid segregation laws and the lack of opportunity, no matter what your qualifications. He was now an ex-soldier who, like millions of others, stood naked before the world while trying to jump-start a life that had been left behind when going off to war. The thought hit him that maybe he was wrong in believing that they were trying to re-start the lives they had known previously. Life for them and for him would never, could never, be the same. Maybe what all of them were trying to do was to invent new lives. Jeff knew immediately that he had to invent a new life for himself. How could he ever go back to being a delivery boy and doing odd jobs?

How could he ever risk his life and the lives of others in behalf of freedom only to come home and readily place himself in a position of servitude? What he was about to do now would give him and perhaps others a new, more fulfilling life grounded in freedom and justice. At the very least, it would give him a life worth living. Mrs. Merrill was right, he concluded, college had a lot to offer him and he began to think that just maybe he had something to offer to the college.

CHAPTER TWENTY-SIX

On the train to Nashville, Jeff was at peace with himself. He started to think about his life. What were the forces that had gotten him this far? It was certain, he thought, that he had not done it alone. It seemed to him that Mama Essie had played a huge role in the drama that was his life. She had taught him basic honesty and the value of striving to be a better person. She had always told him, "Good things come to those who wait." But she had also said, "When good things arrive, don't wait to seize them."

The general, the JAG and the board of officers must have recognized something in him. Otherwise, what could have been a disastrous incident in his life would not have turned into something so special for him. His various commanders had, in many instances, gone out of their way to help him over the rough spots. They had given him more and more responsibility and they had allowed him to carry out that responsibility without interference. In fact, they had made it possible for him to succeed.

Mrs. Merrill had been the anchorperson in his life from the day he walked into the Staten Island library. It seemed to him that she had somehow been waiting for his appearance. Her wise counsel and her determination to guide him through the perilous waters in a sea of changing lifestyles and newfound values made him wonder. Had their meeting been just a lucky encounter or was it somehow destiny? Whatever it was that had caused their paths to cross, he was certainly richer for it. If she really was an angel, she had, he was certain, made heaven proud.

At the admissions office of Tennessee State, two sophomore students met Jeff—a young man, who looked all of seventeen or eighteen, and a young woman, who was poised, articulate and friendly. The two students took him on a tour of the campus and

introduced him to a few veterans of the military who had recently
enrolled in the university. The admissions officer was an obviously
intelligent woman, who immediately put him at ease. She asked
about his background and his aspirations for the future. She was a
good listener and she took a few notes as Jeff struggled to recount
his past and make his hopes for the future clear. At the end of the
interview, she indicated that she was pleased with what she had
heard. She made an appointment for him to see her again the
following morning. Meanwhile, she advised him that he had an
appointment to see the academic dean as soon as he left the
admissions office.

The academic dean was outgoing and very friendly. He was
interested in how Jeff had managed to enter the Army at such a
young age and in what motivated him to take such a drastic step.
The dean talked to Jeff about his aspirations in much the same
manner that the admissions officer had done. He asked Jeff to
imagine himself ten years in the future and to describe what he
saw. When he heard Jeff's reply, he said, "Now let's go ten years
further to twenty years."

As Jeff began to speak, the dean interrupted him briefly and
said, "I want you to speak from you heart, not so much from your
head. I'd like to hear what's in your heart. It may be relatively easy
for the university to change or re-direct what's in your head, but
only you can know what's in your heart."

As he began, Jeff said, "Sir, I'll probably switch back and forth
between what's in my heart and what's in my head. Sometimes
the two intertwine. Just allow me to speak what I feel, sir. Maybe
it will become clear to me which is which.

"I believe I see the need for change in our country. While I was
in the Army, I saw this country embark on the noble pursuit of
freeing Western Europe from the tyranny and the servitude of a
vicious dictator. The irony of this noble undertaking is that a large
number of the people who fought to free Western Europe came
home, dead or severely injured, to a nation that still would not
allow 'their kind' to enjoy the basic freedoms they had helped to
secure for the Europeans."

"What's your point?" the dean asked.

"My point, sir," Jeff continued, "is to question what we, as a people, can do to advance our own quest for freedom. What can I, as an individual, do?"

The dean sat up in his large swivel chair, and looked at Jeff. "Young man," he began, "the questions you are raising are not new. Generations of black people have raised these questions. There is no simple answer. Certainly, the university can help to raise awareness, but it cannot, on its own, secure what we seek. Freedom is an individual and collective idea that must be defined by those who are denied it. But let me caution you, freedom is not now, nor will it ever be free. Freedom comes with a price tag and huge responsibilities. It requires sacrifice, hard work, courage and dedication. It requires devotion and vigilance. Freedom doesn't come in a package tied with a fancy ribbon. If this is your vision, and it should be our vision, be prepared for a long hard struggle. Those who have the power never give it up willingly. You have to seize the power—not through the kind of armed struggle you just recently participated in, but by peaceful, legitimate means. You have to give the power structure reasons to share power. We can do this through the ballot box and by economic means. It will not be done in a decade or a generation. Perhaps it won't be completed in my lifetime or yours, but it can, and it will be achieved. Maybe," the dean went on, "we should place our emphasis on very young people like you. You've been to hell. You know what Armageddon is likely to be like. I believe you are sincere in your desire and willingness to make the sacrifice needed to secure this basic human right."

The dean quickly turned his attention to the reason Jeff was there. "As I understand it," he said, "you're seeking admission to this institution."

"Yes, I am, sir."

"You did not travel the traditional route to get into college?"

"No sir, I did not."

"Your sponsor, or mentor, has great faith in you. She believes that you are uniquely qualified to do college work. Do you believe that?"

"Yes, I do, sir."

The dean looked at Jeff and said, "Based upon the recommendation I have in my hand and the conversation we just finished, I believe it is unnecessary to have you go through the process of taking an admissions test. If it's agreeable to you, I'm going to waive the test. I'll instruct the office of admissions to enroll you, beginning with the academic year that starts in September."

To say that Jeff was surprised by the dean's action was an understatement. He was stunned. He had come to Nashville expecting to take a test about many subjects to which he had never been exposed. He had serious doubts about being able to pass the test, but he was going to give it his best and he was going to fight to be admitted on a probationary basis if he failed to pass. Now, the academic dean had removed this last obstacle to his admission. In two months, he would be a freshman at this university.

Jeff called Mrs. Merrill from the student center to give her the good news. She did not seem surprised at all. She was low key in her congratulations. Her reaction was a disappointment to him.

"You don't seem surprised," he said to her.

"I'm not," she replied. "We've been working toward this day for a long time. We were successful because of the hard work we've done and also because you deserve to be in college. What did you expect?"

"I don't know what I expected," Jeff replied. "I certainly didn't expect that it would be this easy."

Mrs. Merrill exploded. "It was not that easy! The university did you no special favor. You've earned the right to be there or at any other college or university of your choice. I wish you would stop downplaying yourself and realize that you have qualities that many people strive to acquire. Believe in yourself, Jeff! Love yourself, because no one will love you if you don't love yourself."

"Why are you so angry?" Jeff asked.

"I'm not angry."

"You sound angry."

"Well, maybe I am," she said. "Maybe I'm a little jealous that I can't be as patient and as humble as you, after all that you have been through. With my temperament, I'm sure I would have gone crazy and perhaps hurt someone had I been subjected to what you have been forced to endure most, if not all, of your life."

Jeff paused for a moment, holding the phone close to his ear. He was trying to think of a reply to what she had just said. "You're an angel," Jeff said, "and angels don't fight."

"That's not true," she quickly replied. "Sometimes angels are forced to fight."

"I doubt that," Jeff said.

"Where are you staying tonight?" she said

"In a small motel near the campus," Jeff replied.

"Before you go to sleep tonight," she said, "I want you to take the time to read the Book of Revelations. Most hotels and motels have Bibles. Read it, please!"

On the plane back to New York, Jeff tried to put the things that the academic dean and Mrs. Merrill had said into proper perspective. The dean had said that freedom does not come wrapped in a pretty package. You have to be willing to struggle, to sacrifice and, if necessary, to die for it. He did, however, caution that violence was not the way. Mrs. Merrill had suggested that patience, while being a virtue, had its limits. Both the dean and Mrs. Merrill, made good sense to him. He knew how much he abhorred violence. He had seen violence at its worst over the past two years and it was not a sight he ever wanted to see again. Somewhere, there must be a middle position between patience and violence. Maybe Mrs. Merrill and the dean were trying to tell him that it was a part of his duty to help to find that position.

Since coming home from Europe, Jeff had been busy, very busy—spending time with his family in Alabama, going to Nashville to apply for admission to the university and seeing Mrs. Merrill at least three times a week. He felt that he needed a rest. He vowed that for the next month he would do lots of reading, go to the beach and just goof off. There was nothing compelling his attention at this point. All of the necessary application forms for his benefits under the G.I. Bill of Rights had been sent to the Veterans Administration. He had only to show up in September to register for classes. For the first time in his life, Jeff had time on his hands and enough money to do some of the things he had never before had an opportunity to do.

Upon his arrival in New York, he sent Mama Essie a telegram informing her of his acceptance to the university. He was a little pleased that he did not have to tell her in person because he knew that this was an emotional time and subject for her. She had said to Jeff, when he was home, that she and the whole family would be praying for him to be accepted. "No one will ever be able to say that you are not 'somebody'" was the last thing Mama Essie had said to him when he boarded the train for New York. She had tears in her eyes at the prospect of Jeff having a chance at college. Now that his admission was a reality, he could only imagine how emotional this news would be for her. Jeff disliked seeing anyone cry. This was especially true with respect to seeing Mama Essie with her eyes filled with tears, even tears of happiness.

Mrs. Merrill called Aunt Lila and left a message for Jeff to return her call when he arrived in New York. Jeff was stricken with fear. Had something happened to Mrs. Merrill? She had never before called and Aunt Lila said that her voice had a tone of urgency. It was near midnight when the plane landed at LaGuardia Airport and it was much too late to call her when he arrived at Aunt Lila's apartment. As tired as he was, Jeff had difficulty sleeping. He kept wondering about Mrs. Merrill's call. Please God, he thought, don't let anything bad happen to this dear woman. She deserves the best, Lord, Jeff prayed. She is doing your work on Earth.

Promptly at nine the next morning, Jeff phoned Mrs. Merrill at the library. She immediately recognized the anxiety in his voice. "Why are you so upset?" she said.

"I'm worried about you," Jeff responded. "Aunt Lila said your voice had the tone of urgency and it was the first time you ever called me here."

"Settle down, young man," she directed, "I'm fine, but Sal and I have been talking about you."

"You mean you have been talking about me behind my back?" Jeff laughed with a sigh of relief.

"Yes, behind your back," she answered. "Listen to me, Jeff."

"I always listen to you."

Mrs. Merrill began, "Sal and I want you to have dinner with us tonight. We think that there is something that you need to do before you go back to Tennessee to begin your classes."

"What should I do?" Jeff asked.

"Just meet us at the restaurant at seven tonight."

After he hung up the phone, Jeff's mind went into overdrive. What was it that she believed he should do now? Everything that she had told him to do he had done. He had read and studied books he had never heard about. She had introduced him to a few very famous authors. He had, with her help, gotten his high school diploma and he had just been admitted to college. What was it that he had missed?

Aunt Lila said, "You can sit here all day and speculate, but the only way you'll ever know what they think you should do now is to go to the restaurant and hear it for yourself."

On the train downtown, Jeff could think of nothing except Mrs. Merrill's words. "We think that there's something you should do before you go back to Tennessee." These same words haunted him on the ferry ride to Staten Island and in the cab on his way to the restaurant.

The small restaurant was full when he walked in. Mrs. Merrill was seated in the far corner and there was someone with her. The man had his back to Jeff as he approached Mrs. Merrill's table. She started to smile when she saw Jeff. As she stood to greet him, the man also stood. He turned toward Jeff, extended his right hand and said, "I'm Father Morrelli."

Jeff was astonished. Had Mrs. Merrill brought him and Father Morrelli together for the purpose of converting him or did she feel that he had committed a terrible sin and needed to confess? When the introduction was finished, Sal came to the table and handed Jeff a double shot of bourbon.

"Sal," Mrs. Merrill admonished, "do I have to remind you again about that bourbon? You're polluting his mind and his body."

"Relax, Anna Marie," Father Morrelli intoned, "It's not what goes into the body that pollutes, it's what comes out of the body."

This was a refreshing thought to Jeff. He was almost certain that he had read these very words somewhere. Over dinner, there was lots of small talk. Father Morrelli had spent more than two years in the chaplain corps of the Army, serving in the Pacific. He had traveled extensively in the southern part of the United States and he understood and appreciated the things Jeff and his family had endured.

"What you've been through," Father Morrelli said, "is painful to me. I can't begin to imagine how much pain and suffering you've endured."

"Jeff," Mrs. Merrill began, "look at me. Look into my eyes and think deeply about what I'm saying to you. The ghost of the Ku Klux Klan is still embedded deep in your psyche. You may not fully realize it, but, to some extent, they still control you. You sense that they are a mysterious, controlling power but you must come to realize that they are just a bunch of robed hoodlums who depend upon you to give them power. You give them that power by allowing them to put fear into your heart and mind. Take charge of your life. Cast off the fear. See the Klan for what they are. Free yourself from the past. The whole world is before you. Embrace it. Then go out and help others to do the same. I can sit here and talk forever but only you have the power to take control of your life."

Jeff sat just staring at Mrs. Merrill. Even while she was sitting only a foot or two away from him, her eyes and her voice seemed to be coming from a far distance. Jeff had the feeling that he was trying to move, trying to divert his eyes from her eyes, but he seemed powerless to do so. Mrs. Merrill picked up a large white linen napkin from the table and wiped his eyes and his cheeks. Jeff had not realized that he was crying and he felt ashamed. Father Morrelli spoke and it was then that Jeff was able to turn away from Mrs. Merrill.

"What are you feeling, son?" Father Morrelli asked.

"I'm feeling shame," Jeff said.

"About what?"

"About being so emotional in public."

Father Morrelli placed his hand on Jeff's hand and said, "Son, Jesus wept and, because He did, He gave us not only permission to weep, but He gave us reason to weep. 'Each wrong,' he said, 'demands a tear.' What Anna Marie has said to you may sound abstract and complicated, but in reality, it's very simple. You have to take some time to think. After you have done your own thinking, you must act. You must act in your own behalf."

"What are you suggesting I do, Father?"

"You must go back to Jerusalem," Father Morrelli said.

Jeff was stunned by what the priest had said. The tears began to flow again, but he was not ashamed now. He didn't care. "Father, I've never been to the place you call 'Jerusalem'."

"Oh," Father Morrelli said, "you've been there. You just don't realize it now. Everyone has a Jerusalem in their life and they must one day go back and face it if they ever hope to be whole. Your Jerusalem came early in your life. I believe Anna Marie said you were about six years old when the Klan came to your house. I also understand that you have no conscious memory before that incident. Is that correct?"

"That's correct."

"I believe that this experience, this inhumane, devastating experience, still haunts a small part of your consciousness and a large part of your subconscious."

The priest continued. "One day, you're going to have to go back and come face to face with the place where all of this took place. This is your Jerusalem. It may be hard for you to do, but I believe that you have to do it," he finished.

Sal came back to the table and sat another drink before Jeff. Mrs. Merrill did not object this time. As he walked away from the table, Sal whispered in Jeff's ear, "Don't resist what she tells you to do. She has great powers of persuasion and she's very persistent. She won't stop until you accede to her wishes. She's like Gabriel. When she sounds the trumpet, everyone hears the sound."

The three of them sat at the table without a word being spoken for a good five minutes. Finally, Father Morrelli said, "My mission here is finished. I've given you the best advice I can think of. I hope that it will be useful to you, Jeff. Please give this matter your best thoughts. Pray about it, ask your Maker for guidance."

As Father Morrelli rose to leave, he turned to Mrs. Merrill and said, "Anna Marie, the check for his round trip to Alabama is in this envelope. Keep me informed and, if there's anything else that I can do, please call me."

Father Morrelli left the restaurant. Mrs. Merrill tried to give the envelope to Jeff but he refused to take it. He looked at Mrs. Merrill and he spoke very softly. "I am deeply grateful to you for all of the things you have done for me. Where I would have been without you, only God knows. I'll go to Alabama again because, as you have said, I can't heal the wounds inflicted upon me until I've done this. But I have to refuse the money for the train trip. I have enough money and I need to participate in my own healing."

She did not argue this point. "I told Father Morrelli that you would refuse the money, but he felt that we should offer it," she said. "Let me know when you decide the time you'll be leaving."

"I plan to leave right away," Jeff said. "Maybe as early as the day after tomorrow."

On the ferry back to Manhattan, Jeff tried to memorize and to examine every phase of the conversation that had taken place among Mrs. Merrill, Father Morrelli and himself. Would going back to the place of the most traumatic experience of his life help him dispose of the demons of so long ago? The Ku Klux Klan was, indeed, a demon in his life just as it had been a demon in the lives of so many before him. Father Morrelli had said that this was his Jerusalem and that, in order to heal himself, he had to go back. Jeff could now faintly recall some of the biblical stories Grandma Dawson used to tell. She had, if he remembered correctly, one time told the story of Jesus' return to Jerusalem a few days before he was to be crucified. Surely, Father Morrelli was not comparing him to Jesus. The Bible said that Jesus died to atone for our sins and to save the world. Jeff knew that he was going back to Alabama not to save the world, but to try and save himself. He did not understand all of the things that Father Morrelli had said but one thing was clear to him, the Klan had had a devastating effect on his life. They created fear, anger, and hatred. Father Morrelli believed and Jeff hoped that the trip back to the scene of the crime would be the beginning of a healing process.

Aunt Lila called the train station to make Jeff's reservation and she helped him pack his bag for the trip. Jeff had informed Mrs. Merrill of the date and the time of his departure. She did not engage him in conversation as she usually did. Instead, she wished him luck and a safe return to New York.

Jeff arrived at the train station an hour before his scheduled departure. He checked his bag and was reading *The Daily News* when two people sat down next to him. He looked to either side and there sat Mrs. Merrill and Sal. Jeff smiled and said, "Why are you here?"

"Just to offer you our friendship and moral support," she said.

Sal smiled, and said, "We don't feel like talking now, so let's just sit here silently until it's time for you to board the train."

For the next half hour, they sat together in silence. Not a word passed between them. When his train was announced, the three walked to the boarding gate. Sal put out his hand and shook Jeff's hand. Mrs. Merrill took Jeff's hands, looked deep into his eyes and, in a voice that was barely audible, said, "My prayers are with you." Without waiting for Jeff to reply, they turned and quickly walked away.

CHAPTER TWENTY-SEVEN

Jeff had not informed Mama Essie that he would be coming home. He felt it was better this way. He knew that he would have to explain the reason for his trip and he was not yet prepared to do that. On the long train ride south, Jeff was relaxed. He seemed to be at peace with himself and all of his surroundings. He was able to sleep for long periods of time. He felt as if he was about to enter a new phase of life. The anxiety that he felt when he sat in the restaurant with Father Morrelli and Mrs. Merrill was gone. He was ready to go back and face his Jerusalem. Jeff said to himself, "Ku Klux Klan, you no longer have power over me."

Mama Essie was sitting on the front porch when the taxicab carrying Jeff stopped in front of her house. She looked up as Jeff got out of the cab. When she finally realized that the person exiting the cab was her son, she rushed from the porch to meet him. She grabbed his hand and smiled broadly.

"Do you plan to stay until it's time for you to go to school in Tennessee?" she inquired.

"No, Mama," Jeff said, "This trip was somewhat unplanned. I'll only be here for a few days. I'll explain it all to you after we have had our supper."

"Is there trouble?" Mama Essie asked.

"No, Mama. There's no trouble. Everything is fine and I hope it will be even better before I leave."

Mama Essie asked no more questions. She went about the task of cooking supper and bringing Jeff up to date about the family and activities in the town.

"People around here are very surprised that you'll be going to college in September," Mama Essie said with pride.

"Are you surprised, Mama?" Jeff asked.

"No, I'm not surprised," she answered. "You have what it takes to do anything you want. Just be sure that you do what's best for you."

"Haven't I always tried to do that, Mama?" Jeff inquired.

"No, son, I don't believe you've always done that. When you left home to join the Army, it was because you wanted to help to make a better life for us. You gave almost all of the money you earned during these years in the Army to us. Now, I think it's time for you to do something for yourself."

Jeff immediately tried to change the subject. He was uncomfortable talking about the things he had tried to do for his family, but Mama Essie was not yet finished. "I don't want you to feel that you have to ignore your own needs to take care of us," she continued. "We're better off now than we've ever been in our lifetime. Now you have to go to the university and do what's in your best interest."

"I will, Mama," Jeff began, "but I hope that you aren't telling me to forget the family, because if you are, I'll never be able to do that."

"No, I'm not telling you that," she said. "I'm telling you that your success is our success. When you do well, you bless us all."

After supper, Mama Essie lost no time inquiring about the reason Jeff had come back home so soon after his last visit.

"Mama Essie," Jeff began, "I came back home because there's something I need to do—something I must do in order to clear my mind and close a chapter in our lives that has affected me deeply. I'm sure that it's had an effect upon you also."

Mama Essie's face became very tense. The veins in her forehead were visible in a way that he had not noticed before. She folded her hands to prevent them from trembling and she looked into Jeff's eyes without blinking. "Do we have trouble?" she asked quietly. "What is it that you have to do?"

"Mama," Jeff said, "I have to go back to that place where the Klan came that night."

"But that was years ago," Mama Essie protested, "You can't do anything about that now. Forget it, son. Forget it. Go on to college;

don't rekindle the past. Let sleeping dogs lie. As long as they're asleep," she whispered, "they can't bite you."

"That's the point, Mama. The dogs are not sleeping. They're lying in wait, ready to attack with or without provocation. I have to do this, Mama," Jeff said. "You just told me to do what's in my best interest. I hope that you'll believe me when I tell you that this is in my best interest."

"What do you expect to see out there?" Mama Essie asked, "The Klan won't be there. All that this will do is remind you of a terrible incident that happened a long time ago. Don't torture yourself. Let it go. Look ahead," she said. "There's nothing back there that can harm you now."

Jeff was not prepared for the intensity of Mama Essie's reaction. Just the thought of that horrible night left her trembling. Her eyes were filled with fear.

"Mama, I'm not suggesting that you go back there. I'm only saying to you that I have to go. This is my Jerusalem and I have to face it alone. No, Mama, the Klan won't be there. But the grounds, the woods and, maybe, remnants of the house will be there. I just need to be able to tell myself that I came back and that I left all of my fears and hatred where they originated."

Mama Essie was not pleased with Jeff's decision but he believed that she understood his burning desire, his compelling need, to go back to that awful place.

When Jeff awoke the next morning Mama Essie was gone. A note next to the coffee pot said, "I've gone to see about a car for you." Indeed, Mama Essie did know that this was something that he had to do. When she returned, her face was gaunt, but her voice was clear and steady. She spoke rapidly, but with clarity of purpose.

"Reverend Mack will give you his car tonight," Mama Essie said, "You can use it for as long as you want." Over two cups of coffee, she related the conversation she had had with Reverend Mack.

"The reverend," she told Jeff, "understood why you had to return to that place to confront your fears and conquer them." He had told Mama Essie that this need on Jeff's part might be a spiritual calling from God. It could be, he told her, that this was the beginning of a higher mission that God had in mind for Jeff. Whatever it was, he was in favor of Jeff going back out there. In fact, he encouraged it. Mama Essie was calmer now. Much of her fear had been alleviated because of her talk with Reverend Mack.

"When do you plan to go?" Mama Essie asked Jeff.

"Tonight," he said. "Late tonight."

"Why late at night?" Mama Essie inquired.

"Because they came late at night," Jeff answered. "I want to synchronize my arrival with the time of their arrival. "Do you remember what time they came, Mama?"

"I'll never forget," she answered. "It was twenty minutes before midnight."

At eight o'clock that night, Jeff went to Reverend Mack's home to get the car. The reverend offered a short prayer and gave him the keys. "Keep the car overnight," he said, "and let me know if you need me. What you're about to do is right and proper," he said. "I know that the Lord will be with you out there. You don't have to be afraid."

Jeff drove the car back to Mama Essie's house. They drank coffee and they waited. The trip to the scene of his fear was about nine miles out into the heart of nowhere. If the scene was still the way it used to be, there would be large cotton fields and acres upon acres of corn, peanuts, and vegetables. At about eleven o'clock, when Jeff was ready to leave, Mama Essie hugged him and asked if he was carrying a gun.

"No, Mama," he smiled, "I left guns behind when I came home from Europe. Jesus didn't have a weapon when he returned to Jerusalem."

On the drive to the plantation, Jeff was deep in thought. Would the old shack they called a house still be there? What about the big pecan tree in the center of the yard, the tree that they were going to use to hang his father? Would it be there? Were there people living in the old shack, if it was still standing? What would his reaction be when he finally saw the place again?

Driving along the red dirt roads, his heart started to pound almost out of control as he drew near the scene. Jeff knew that, if discovered, he could be arrested for trespassing by the sheriff. He also knew that, in spite of this possibility, this was a mission he had to complete. This was a ghost from his past and the ghost would continue to haunt him until they came face to face.

Jeff touched the high beam light switch with his left foot and he saw the big pecan tree in the center of the yard. The knot in his stomach almost caused him to lose control of the car, but he quickly regained control of his emotions and guided the car into the big yard. The midnight moon hung in the sky like a brightly colored kite over still water. The night was hot and there was no hint of wind stirring anywhere in the area. Slowly, Jeff got out of the car, looked in the direction of the house and started to move slowly toward it. It did not appear to him that anyone lived in the rundown house, but he could not be certain unless he moved closer. Standing near what had once been the wooden steps to the front porch, he was convinced that the house was vacant. The wooden boards of the porch were rotted and the window shutters were dangling loosely on their rusty hinges. Jeff walked around to the side and the back. It was clear that no one had lived here in the recent past. Although the house was abandoned, the fields on either side of the house were brimming with cotton plants, corn, and peanuts.

The sounds that emanated from deep in the woods behind this broken house took Jeff back to the days of his boyhood when he would sit on the front porch after supper and listen to the sounds of the crickets, the night birds, and the hoot owls. These were the same sounds he now heard on this hot August night.

Jeff returned to the car and drove to a spot in the back yard near a window where his father had escaped the clutches of the Klan. From this spot, he knew that he was sheltered from observation by anyone passing by. As he sat in the car, he tried to bring into focus all of the memories of that night. He tried desperately to close his mind to the night noises around him and to re-create the events of that terrible experience. He could vividly recall how he and his family were awakened from a deep sleep by the sounds of chaotic activity in the yard surrounding the house.

Grandma Dawson was the first to hear the noises and she promptly alerted the rest of family. Jeff and his brothers and sisters opened the wooden shutters to the windows and saw a huge wooden cross burning in the center of the yard.

When Grandma Dawson opened the front door, she came face to face with four hooded Klansmen. "Where's that nigger Clem?" they demanded.

"I don't know where the nigger is," Grandma Dawson replied, "but if I find him before you good white folks find him, he's a dead nigger."

"When did you last see him?" one Klansman shouted.

"About first night," she said. "He was drunk and he left here headed toward town."

"If he returns, will you let us know?" the Klansman demanded.

"Yes, sir," Grandma Dawson replied. "Where will I find you, sir?"

"Just tell any white man you see and we'll come out here. Do you understand what you have to do, Aunt Clara?"

"Yes, sir. I know what to do, but I'm telling you now, by the time you get here the nigger'll be dead. I'll kill him myself."

"All right, Aunt Clara, go back to bed. No harm will come to you."

The Klansmen returned to the yard and joined the group of about twenty robed men who had begun a solemn, ritualistic ceremony as they circled the burning cross, holding their shotguns. The leader shouted, "Let's go, boys. We'll get this nigger later."

It was at this point that Jeff recalled something that had escaped his memory all of these years. Jeff now remembered seeing a young boy dressed in full Klan regalia. The boy appeared to be about eight or perhaps nine years old. The leader said to the boy, "Let's go home, son."

"I don't want to go home, Daddy," the boy cried. "You broke your promise. You said you'd let me help kill a nigger tonight."

"You'll get your chance to kill lots of niggers, son. The one we were looking for tonight got away, but we'll get him later. I promise you, I'll let you shoot him after we string him up."

"You promise, Daddy?" the boy pleaded.

"I promise, son. I promise."

Jeff shuddered at the memory.

When the Klansmen left, Grandma Dawson gathered the family around her and told them that she had suspected there would be trouble over the bale of cotton Jeff's father had sold, so she stayed awake while the family slept. When she heard movement in the distance, she alerted Jeff's father. He quickly got dressed and escaped by climbing out of a back window and running quickly into the woods. Jeff knew that Grandma Dawson's brave charade that night had saved his father's life.

Jeff sat in the car behind the rundown house for what seemed to him like an eternity. Were there other things about that night that he had also forgotten? He tried to force his brain to release any other information that had been buried there, long forgotten, but nothing came.

Jeff got out of the car, walked slowly toward the front yard and stood under the big pecan tree. A chill ran through his body as he stood silently, almost prayerfully, under the big tree. It could have ended here. He tried not to remember that this tree could have seen the end of his father's life. Except for Grandma Dawson's wisdom and quick thinking, it would have been the end.

Jeff had never seen anyone hanging by the neck from a tree, but he had seen other forms of intimidating violence. On two occasions, he had seen adult black men shot, tied with ropes and dragged behind cars through the black or "Negro" sections of town. This practice served as a solemn reminder to all "Negroes" that this was the price they would pay if they dared step out of line— a line that was set by whites and sometimes changed on a whim to suit the purpose of the moment.

Jeff looked at his watch; it was almost two o'clock in the morning. He had been here more than two hours. Where had the time gone? It seemed to him that he had just arrived. As he walked back toward the car, he suddenly found himself walking fast, in a zigzag pattern. He realized that this was how soldiers in combat areas move in order to avoid a sniper's direct shot. He knew that there was no need for this kind of defensive action now. This was not a combat area and there were no snipers lurking in the bushes or behind the trees. Or were there? This place, just a few years earlier, had been designated a killing ground. These very grounds were to be the place where his father would be hung from the big tree, the place where an eight—or nine-year-old boy would have fulfilled his desire to follow in his Klan father's footsteps by aiming a twelve-gauge shotgun and helping to snuff out the life of a man whose highest ambition was to feed his large family.

As he sat in the car behind the house, Jeff was filled with shame that he had become so frightened when he walked back toward the car. He realized that he had not even been quite this scared on the beach at Normandy or in the Battle of the Bulge. Maybe, Jeff thought, maybe this was the Klan's greatest and only strength. Fear and intimidation are powerful weapons. Because of their secret societies and their ability to instill fear, the Klan often exercised complete control over their enemies. They came at midnight, dressed in robes and hoods, carrying shotguns, rifles, and ropes for hanging. Their black victims were almost always taken by surprise. They were unarmed and often clueless as to the reasons they were being sought. In many instances, they were murdered in an atmosphere of drunken festivity, with the knowledge and participation of the police and sheriff's departments.

Being scared at Normandy and during the Battle of the Bulge was a different kind of fear. You knew who the enemy was and you knew his approximate location. You knew why you were fighting him. The enemy was heavily armed and so were you. Strategy, for the most part, dictated the outcome of the fight. There were rules of engagement and the two sides met as equals. Such was not the case with the Klan. There were no rules of engagement. The Klan knew you, but you never knew them. They could be anybody— your local grocer, the policeman or sheriff, the clerk at the bank or, sometimes, the local preacher. They were always heavily armed. They used the element of surprise and they often outnumbered their lone victim by as many as fifty to one. They did their evil deeds, removed their hoods and robes, and blended back into the community as law-abiding citizens.

Yes, the Klan ruled by fear and played by their own rules. Take away the fear and they lose the ability to control.

Sitting there in the car, Jeff started to feel that he understood the dynamics of the fear that had never really left him. He got out of the car, looked toward the heavens and quietly said, "The Lord is my Shepherd and I shall not fear." He got back into the car and headed toward Mama Essie's house. He had come back to his Jerusalem and he knew now that he had entered a new phase of his life.

CHAPTER TWENTY-EIGHT

When Jeff parked the car in front of Mama Essie's house, it was four thirty the next morning. He had spent more than four hours at that place. All of the lights were on in the house. Mama Essie had not gone to bed while he was away. Jeff knew that she was worried about him going to that place, but he had not expected her to remain up all night. As soon as he walked in, she said, "I'll make some coffee for us."

Once again, over cups of coffee, Jeff shared his experiences and insights with his mother. She listened intently and nodded her head with understanding and approval. When Jeff finished talking, Mama Essie spoke softly, "Now we can both get some sleep."

They slept until almost ten o'clock the following day. When they awoke, the August heat was oppressive. After returning the car to Reverend Mack, Jeff sat with his mother in the welcome shade of the front porch. She told Jeff that she knew the little boy had been present that night. She could even identify the boy and his father. She had recognized their voices. A few weeks before the incident, she had done some dressmaking for the boy's mother. Mama Essie said it would have been suicidal to let the boy's family know that she recognized them, so she had kept quiet about the incident. Jeff asked Mama Essie if she, too, would like to go out to that place, to confront it and dispense with the past, but her answer was an emphatic, "No. Never."

As they sat on the porch, Jeff's thoughts drifted from the past to the future. It was now a matter of weeks before he would enter college in Tennessee. He knew that he must focus on this new challenge. He would not enter college as a conventional student. Unlike most of the hundreds of freshmen students, he had not had the benefit of going through elementary school and high school.

College would be a major change in his life, one that he could not have anticipated as he struggled to grow up in Alabama.

In spite of the promise that his future held, Jeff was having trouble putting the past completely behind him. As he continued to recall the words of the little boy, he was deeply troubled. The little boy would be an adult now. What were his thoughts? Would he carry on the tradition and the actions of his father? Did he now have children of his own? Would he, like his father, promise his children that they would be given the "privilege" of helping to kill a nigger?

The big pecan tree that sat in the center of the yard continued to cause pain in Jeff's heart. He continued to see this tree as a symbol of what could have happened that night had it not been for the insight of Grandma Dawson. What bothered Jeff as much as anything else was the father's indoctrination of the little boy. If the boy upheld his father's tradition, this would ensure that a new generation of violent Klansmen would emerge.

Mama Essie was aware of the effect that the previous night's trip had had on him. She continued to try to move his thoughts from the past to the future, a future that she knew held such promise for him. She reminded him that not all people were like the Klan. She cited Mrs. Merrill and Father Morrelli as examples. She truly believed that four years at college would help him to put his experiences in perspective and to find a satisfactory and constructive path forward

"If," Mama Essie said, "you see a problem, you have to find a way to solve the problem. Don't forget what you've seen," she continued, "but go on to the university and study hard. Be determined that you and others will find a way to solve some of the problems that trouble us."

Three days had passed since Jeff arrived back home to face his Jerusalem. He had deliberately waited for his emotions to subside before he called Mrs. Merrill and Father Morrelli. He knew that they expected to hear from him, but he wanted to tell them about his trip to that place without becoming emotionally overwrought. He now felt that he could talk to them calmly and give them some insight into what he felt and how the experience had affected him. Because Mama Essie did not have a phone, Reverend Mack offered the use of the telephone at the church. Reverend Mack said Jeff could talk as long as he needed to talk. "This is," he said, "an important call and a meaningful way for the church to aid a suffering soul."

At ten o'clock in the morning, Jeff placed the call to Mrs. Merrill at the Staten Island library. When she came on the line, it was obvious to Jeff that she was excited and anxious to hear from him. Mrs. Merrill asked him to hold his remarks a little longer. She believed that it was important for Father Morrelli to be a part of their conversation. She asked Jeff to give her a telephone number where she and Father Morrelli could call him back at seven o'clock that evening. Reverend Mack welcomed Jeff to receive the call there and promised that the church would be open at the agreed upon time.

Promptly at seven o'clock, the call from Mrs. Merrill and Father Morrelli came. They were calling from the church where Father Morrelli was the pastor; the priest was on an extension. The thought entered Jeff's mind that some powerful forces were at work here. This important call was being made between two churches, hundreds of miles apart, arranged by two pastors who did not know each other. In fact, they had never even heard of each other. Jeff suspected that Father Morrelli had acted on some unique and special insight when he had encouraged, pleaded and, in the end, almost demanded that Jeff come back to this place, at this time, to meet what the priest called his "Jerusalem".

After Father Morrelli extended a warm greeting to Jeff, he asked Jeff to set the scene for his visit to that place. Jeff began by telling the priest and Mrs. Merrill about his approach to the house—the hard, red dirt road; the fields of cotton, corn and peanuts on either side and in the back of the house; the big sprawling pecan tree that stood like a monument to evil, spreading its branches over the yard. Then there was the house itself. The house was empty now and it reflected years of neglect. The porch was missing boards and the steps to the porch had fallen down. The wooden shutters on the window were broken. They seemed perilously close to leaving their hinges and falling to the ground. The tin roof was loose and rust covered. The house itself seemed to have shifted on its foundation as it leaned several degrees to the side. The front yard was clean. It looked as if the wind had swept it in preparation for his visit. In back of the house, tall weeds and blackberry bushes grew wild. In the kitchen, where his family had once eaten their meals, the long wooden table was still in place, though one of its legs had fallen through the rotting floor. The entire scene was a reminder of how things used to be.

Father Morrelli asked Jeff if he thought the trip to Alabama and that place had been worthwhile, if it had given him new insights into a past that had plagued him for so long. Jeff never answered the priest's question. It was as if he had not even heard it. Instead, he immediately began to share his recollection of the conversation between the boy and his father. Jeff told Father Morrelli how disappointed the boy had been because he had been promised that he would be allowed to help kill a nigger.

"How old was this boy?"

"I can't be certain, Father, but judging by his voice and his size, he was between eight and ten years old."

"Since the Klan came to kill your father anyway, what was so disturbing to you about the boy's comment?" the priest asked.

Jeff could feel his temperature begin to rise. His body felt like boiling water was running through his veins. His voice started to rise toward a fever pitch. "What was so disturbing about the boy?" Jeff shouted into the phone.

"Yes!" Father Morrelli shouted back.

Instead of infuriating him further, Father Morrelli's shout had a calming influence. Jeff instantly realized that Father Morrelli was on his side; that he was endeavoring to help Jeff think clearly, to cleanse his spirit of any hatred or inclination toward violence that may be lingering within.

Jeff spoke to Father Morrelli more calmly now. "Father," he said, "what was so disturbing about the boy was that he was a child being taught to carry on the evil deed of his elders. What does this say about the future? If we allow this kind of behavior to continue, we could very well duplicate the behavior the world saw in Nazi Germany in the nineteen thirties."

"Go on," Father Morrelli urged. "What about Nazi Germany, in your mind, can be compared to what you and your family experienced that night?"

"Ours was not an isolated case," Jeff said. "The violence visited upon us was a part of a violent life visited upon thousands of black families all over the South."

"But you mentioned the behavior in Nazi Germany. What is there in your mind to compare that night and that place to Nazi Germany?"

"Not just that night, Father, but the thousands of nights preceding that night. No one, no white person spoke up. No group had the courage to say, 'Stop the violence, this is wrong.' The model for this little boy was his father wearing a white robe with a hood, carrying a rope and a shotgun, looking to hang a nigger."

"Come to the point," the priest said. "How, in the name of God, does this relate to Nazi Germany?"

"Hitler organized a youth movement," Jeff said, "a movement made up of children. He taught them violence in all forms. Those youth gangs grew up to be adults and they cherished their violent ways. The German citizens, the people at large, stood silently by; no group or organization had the courage to speak out. We know the results of this inaction, don't we, Father?"

"You tell me," the priest said.

Jeff felt his anger out of control again. He shouted into the phone. "The result was the slaughter of more than six million human beings called 'Jews', the deaths of hundreds of thousands of soldiers from American families and from families around the world. Even with the concentration camps emptied, and the weapons of war silenced, many of us from my generation, and especially from my race, feel that we still have another, equally important, fight to finish. How, Father, do we ask one race of people to fight to bring freedom to another race of people when the race being freed, in many instances, cares little or nothing about the freedoms being denied their liberators?"

"Freedom" Father Morrelli said, "is not always physical. I don't take physical freedom lightly, but freedom is a matter of the spirit. No one can enslave you without some cooperation from you. I don't mean to say that the four million blacks who were held captive for more than three hundred years submitted to such treatment willingly. One is truly a slave only when he or she believes himself or herself to be a slave. The Good Book states clearly that 'you shall know the truth and the truth will set you free'. I'm not at all sure, at this point, that you know the truth. And if you do know the truth, I wonder if you are willing to accept all of the ramifications that this truth brings with it. I don't expect you to answer that question now. It requires a great deal of thought. But, in the past, you have shown yourself to be a thoughtful person."

"We have a moral dilemma here at home, Father," Jeff said.

"Indeed, we do," the priest replied.

Mrs. Merrill continued to question Jeff. "Do you feel that your heart and your soul are sufficiently cleansed that you can put aside the past and concentrate on your studies at the university?"

"Yes, for now. But I have a feeling that the past is only temporarily behind me."

"When will you return to New York?" Mrs. Merrill inquired.

"Within a week," Jeff answered.

After the phone call, Jeff thanked Reverend Mack for his kindness and for his generosity. On the half-mile walk back to Mama Essie's house, Jeff felt a sense of liberation. The problems with the Ku Klux Klan would continue for a long time, but he had liberated his heart and his soul from the fear and the mysticism of the Klan. They were just a group of hate-filled, violent men who depended upon fear to spread their violent philosophy.

Mama Essie said she could sense a change in Jeff after his visit to that place and his telephone conversation with Father Morrelli and Mrs. Merrill. She said he was more relaxed; he seemed to be at peace with himself. Over the next six days before departing for New York, Jeff's conversation was lighthearted and casual. His mother looked forward to the day, four years in the future, when he would graduate from college and begin a new life, prepared to face the changes in society that many agreed must come. Mama Essie said that she was not certain that these changes would come in her lifetime, but she was convinced that they would come in Jeff's lifetime.

As Jeff boarded the train for his trip back to New York, Mama Essie sternly admonished him to remember his past, but to work hard to secure his future. "When you secure your own future," she said, "you can then turn your attention to the future of others."

On the train headed for New York, Jeff put the past behind him and he concentrated his thoughts on the time and energy that would be required to successfully complete four years of intensive college study. He made a list of the things he would need to take to Tennessee. He made note of the reading he still had to do. He had three weeks and four days before he had to be on campus. Jeff knew that these days leading up to his departure for Tennessee would be filled with frenzied activity. He would meet with Father Morrelli at least one more time and he suspected that Mrs. Merrill would want to give him additional advice and insight about what to expect when he finally arrived at the university. He looked forward to meeting with Mrs. Merrill. Her wisdom and her insight served to quell many of his anxieties.

Aunt Lila was pleased that his trip to Alabama had been a success. Mrs. Merrill had called the day before and left a message for Jeff to call her as soon as he arrived. Jeff placed the call immediately. When she answered the phone, he knew that something was not right.

"You have to see Father Morrelli right away," she said. "He's hospitalized and he feels that he may not survive."

Jeff was stunned. "What happened? He seemed fine when we spoke on the phone a week ago."

"He's had another heart attack," Mrs. Merrill said. "He has a long history of problems with his heart. He insisted that you come to visit him at the hospital as soon as possible. When can you meet me there?"

"In about two hours," Jeff answered.

On the train downtown, Jeff started to realize how frail and uncertain life could be. Here was a good man, a man of God, who only desired to do good works. Now he may be on his way to the grave. A feeling of anger was beginning to swell inside him. It just seemed so unfair that a man like Father Morrelli had to suffer while the likes of the Klan seemed to live forever. Under his breath, Jeff prayed for Father Morrelli. "God, I know you have a plan, but I don't understand that plan. I hope you'll help me to understand why Father Morrelli suffers and evil people seem to prosper."

Jeff met Mrs. Merrill at the library. She explained the problems Father Morrelli had suffered over the years with his heart. This attack, she explained, was a little more severe than previous attacks. But the priest had insisted that he wanted to speak to Jeff about his trip to Alabama. He wanted to know more about how Jeff had reacted to his Jerusalem.

"Maybe we should wait a few days until Father Morrelli is better," Jeff said to Mrs. Merrill.

"No," she replied, "he wants us to come now."

The cab ride to the hospital was made in complete silence. Jeff was uncertain about what his emotional reaction would be when he saw Father Morrelli lying in a hospital bed, gravely ill. He could sense Mrs. Merrill's concern because she spoke in a low, soft tone and she refused to look directly at Jeff.

Upon their arrival at the hospital, they went to the cardiac unit where a nurse told them that they would have to speak to Father Morrelli's doctor before they would be allowed to enter his room. Several minutes later, the doctor entered the waiting area. He said the priest was gravely ill and should not be speaking to anyone. "However," the doctor went on, "he insists that he be allowed to see the two of you. You have fifteen minutes. You must ask no questions and you must restrain your emotions while in the room. Listen. Let him do all of the talking. A nurse will be standing by just in case she's needed."

The doctor looked Jeff in the eyes and he said, "Do you understand?"

"Yes," Jeff replied, "but this will be hard."

"It will be hard," the doctor said, "but you must do it."

Over the past two years, Jeff had seen soldiers lying on the fields of combat, wounded and dying. He thought he was prepared for almost anything dealing with life and death, but this was different. He felt first his knees and then his whole body go weak. He began to lose his balance.

"Sit down," the doctor said. "Take as much time as you need to compose yourself. You're a strong young man and this is not the first time you've looked death in the face. Father Morrelli is far better off than you and I. He is at complete peace with himself and with his God. What he wants most now is to pass on to you the peace and well-being that he is experiencing. Physically, Father Morrelli is very sick, but spiritually, he's at his peak. We should all strive to be as spiritually well as the father. You may go in now, but let him do all of the talking."

Jeff and Mrs. Merrill entered the hospital room and they gazed into Father Morrelli's beaming face. He managed to stretch out his hands, one to each of them. They said nothing, waiting for the priest to speak.

He said, "You've been back to your Jerusalem and I'm sure that you're better off now than before you went. Facing one's personal Jerusalem is never easy. It was not intended to be. The Master intended it to be a period of cleansing, a period of redemption. Now that this is done, you can go on to do your life's work, whatever that work may be. You don't have to be afraid anymore. Go about your work and be afraid of nothing, not even death. Keep uppermost in your mind that death is not the end. If you love God, it is the beginning. Do whatever your conscience tells you is best, but I would urge you to think about doing something that involves children. It is, perhaps, too late for some in the older generation to change. But the children will carry your message from one generation to the next. You will live on forever through the children. One caution, be sure that the message you give to the children is a message that pleases the greatest of all message givers. Now," Father Morrelli concluded, "go in peace, and don't look back."

The nurse spoke softly to the two of them. "You must go now. The father needs rest, lots of rest."

Jeff stood rigidly, staring at Father Morrelli, who seemed to drift off into another place. The priest's face shone like the beginning of a new moon and there seemed to be a halo surrounding his head. If this was an illusion, it was an illusion that he would never forget.

"Please," the nurse urged, "you must leave now."

Jeff wanted to take that first step, but he knew that any movement on his part would cause him to fall to the floor. The bottoms of his feet had no feeling at all and his legs felt as if they had fallen asleep. The last few words the priest had spoken were swirling in his head. Jeff was, at that moment, incapable of moving. The nurse left the room briefly and she came back with two attendants. The attendants brought him to a small office behind the nursing station where the doctor was waiting. The nurse took his temperature and his blood pressure. The doctor placed a stethoscope to his heart. "Everything is normal," the doctor announced. "Just sit here for a few minutes and you'll be able to leave."

The doctor and the nurse left the room, leaving Jeff and Mrs. Merrill alone. He looked at Mrs. Merrill and saw the tears streaming down her face. "Why are you crying?" Jeff asked. "Father Morrelli is in good hands and I'm all right. Don't cry for either of us."

She raised her head, placed her right hand under Jeff's chin, looked into his eyes and said, "I'm not crying for Father Morrelli and I'm not crying for you. I'm crying for me. Two of the people closest to me are about to leave me. Father Morrelli will be in heaven within a few hours and you'll be in Tennessee in two weeks. That leaves me alone. Don't I have a right to cry if I wish?"

"You have that right," Jeff answered. "But you're one of God's brightest angels. You will never be alone."

Father Morrelli died in his sleep at two minutes past midnight. Mrs. Merrill called Jeff early on the day of the priest's death. Though he knew that this news would come soon, it did not lessen the pain he felt. Aunt Lila was aware of all that had happened and she very discreetly left the apartment and went to Brooklyn, leaving Jeff to grieve privately.

As he sat at the kitchen table, trying to down hot cups of coffee, he attempted to make sense of all that had happened. Why did Father Morrelli have to leave so soon? He was only fifty-one years old and he was a good man. He placed the welfare of others ahead of his own welfare. Why? What was the logic behind God's thinking? In his sadness and grief, Jeff allowed his mind to drift back to a time when he was a child. He thought that he could hear Mama Essie singing an old song that she loved and often sang, "I didn't come here for to stay." The song made sense now; it made lots of sense. Father Morrelli didn't come here for to stay, and he was the first to recognize it. The priest knew that he was leaving and he wanted to tie up all loose ends. Jeff was the final tie he wanted to make.

"Who am I," Jeff thought, "to question what was inevitable on the day Father Morrelli was born? He knew, better than anyone, that he 'didn't come here for to stay'."

Father Morrelli's funeral mass reflected his life and his work. It was upbeat and positive. It was a tribute to the man that he was. As he was leaving the cemetery, Jeff realized that, although Father Morrelli didn't come here for to say, his legacy did.

CHAPTER TWENTY-NINE

Jeff had two weeks remaining before leaving for Tennessee. He had to finish all of the reading material Mrs. Merrill had given him and he had to shop for clothes. This was a new experience to be sure. As a child, he never had new clothing. All of his young life had been spent in the Army, wearing military attire. Now he had to change to civilian attire. Mrs. Merrill had suggested that she go shopping with him and he welcomed her offer. He knew nothing about buying clothing and he needed all of the help he could get.

The week after Father Morrelli died, Mrs. Merrill, Jeff, and Sal met at the restaurant. It meant a lot to Jeff for the three of them to meet in this familiar setting. He realized that this would be the last time in the foreseeable future that they would be together. But even more important was the feeling that they could somehow make sense of Father Morrelli's death. Although he had not known Father Morrelli as well as he knew Sal and Mrs. Merrill, the priest had had a very profound effect on his life. How could he ever forget that Father Morrelli had been responsible for his going back to Alabama and spending time at that place. Facing "his Jerusalem", as the father had called it, gave Jeff a direct insight into his soul. What he had been and what he now had become was very much related to that place and that night. Jeff realized how much Father Morrelli had meant to him.

Over dinner, Sal started to say something about Father Morrelli, but Mrs. Merrill stopped him in mid-sentence. "Later, Sal," she said firmly. The three of them talked about all of the things they had been through together. Mrs. Merrill said it was time for her to cut the apron strings that had bound Jeff to her and her to him.

"This," she continued, "does not mean that I love you any

less. It means that my love for you dictates that I let you go. I have watched a young soldier grow into a competent, secure young man. Now it's time for you to step out of my shadow, to begin to see the world through your own eyes. Don't be afraid to make mistakes," she said, "mistakes are a part of our lives. We grow and we learn from our mistakes. Be true to your conscience and know that the biggest debt that you owe is to yourself."

Jeff was prepared for her to continue, but Sal placed his hands on hers and stopped her. "Your message is duly noted, Anna Marie," Sal said. "Like Father Morrelli, a part of you will live on and on. Jeff will tell his children and his grandchildren about you. Your legacy is written in our hearts."

Jeff sat at the table, speechless. There were so many thoughts pounding through his head that he knew he could not put into words. Sal looked at him and said, "You don't have to say anything. She knows how you feel and what's in your heart."

After two busy days of shopping for clothing and the other things he needed for his new life as a freshman college student, the pace of Jeff's life seemed to settle back into that of a quieter existence. He spent lots of time with Aunt Lila and he spoke to Mrs. Merrill by phone each day. She was friendly, but she seemed subdued. Over the phone, she told Jeff that he should relax, meditate and prepare his mind for the new life ahead. The transformation from being a soldier to being a college student was a big step, she reminded him. "Relax, get your mind focused and dedicate yourself to college life, just as you dedicated yourself to the life of a soldier."

Over the next week, Jeff did relax. Except for getting his bags packed for shipment to Tennessee, he spent his time reading and re-reading the catalogues and other material about college. It was easy for him to concentrate and focus on the many things that would be required of him in his new civilian role. Over the past four and one half years in the United States Army he was considered a man, he had been treated like a man. All of his thinking skills had been honed by the military. He knew little or nothing about acting or thinking in any other way. He had gone into the Army as a child and he had emerged a man. What could have been a childhood was lost to him forever the day he was sworn into the Army. At this point, he had no time or desire to look back and wonder about what might have been.

The day before he was to leave New York for Tennessee, Jeff received a call from Mrs. Merrill inviting him to have dinner with her. Jeff was extremely pleased with her invitation. Throughout the week, he had wondered just how he would say goodbye to her. Now he was relieved that, once again, they would meet at Sal's place, the small restaurant where he felt so comfortable. He also knew that he must try and hold his emotions in check. Jeff was acutely aware that the one person most responsible for him boarding the train in two days was Anna Marie Merrill. She had stood with him. She had believed in him when even he had doubts. If he had a bright future, it was due, in large part, to the fact that she had been a part of his past.

Jeff wanted to express his feelings, to tell her how much she meant to him. How could a few words express what he felt deep down in his soul? Jeff continued to feel that some force that he had been unable to identify had brought them together. Each time he had tried to identify and examine what he considered this mystical force, he became more frustrated.

Nothing in his background would have predicted such an honest and decent relationship between them. Before going into the United States Army, Jeff could barely remember ever speaking to a white woman except to say, "yes, ma'am," or "no, ma'am" when making a delivery to a home or office in his small home town. Now he was about to say goodbye to this woman who had profoundly changed his life. She had looked at his color and she had gone beyond it. She had examined his ignorance about the world around him and she set out to turn his quest for knowledge into a love of learning. She knew that he was black, but to her it did not matter. To her, he was a miracle of creation and this creation transcended all else.

How could he possibly go to this dinner meeting and not become emotional? Without this woman, would other forces have converged and brought about the same result in his life? In Jeff's mind, it was doubtful. While he knew that there were people he had met during his military service who wished him well, they were busy trying to advance their own lives and careers. Mrs. Merrill was different. Her career was on track and she was at peace with herself. She seemed to thrive on helping others. This was especially true when it came to Jeff. On many occasions, Jeff had thought of her as being an angel. Perhaps she was an angel sent to guide him to his ultimate destiny. Whatever the answer, she was one of a kind and he was a better person because of the interest she had taken in him.

For this last meeting with Mrs. Merrill, Jeff decided that he would just show up for dinner. Whatever happened would just happen. No matter how hard he tried to keep his feelings to himself, Mrs. Merrill always seemed to know what he was feeling and what he was thinking. Maybe showing his emotional side was not all that bad.

Jeff arrived at the restaurant a half hour early. Sal directed him to a table and brought drinks for the two of them. Jeff was pleased that he and Sal would have a chance to talk before Mrs. Merrill arrived. Sal was in a talkative mood. He warned Jeff to allow Mrs. Merrill to talk as much as she wished.

"She is very emotional right now," Sal said. "The only way she'll be able to hold herself together is by continuing to talk. You're special to her. This is the first time in her life that she's been able to plant a seed and watch it grow beyond her wildest imagination. She has always been a volunteer for good causes. She has always tried to help others. This experience has been different. You're different. In spite of the abuse heaped upon you and your family over the years, you've maintained your dignity and you're free of hate. Your attitude and your capacity to see something positive in each person are what impress Anna Marie most. She constantly talks about the impact you can have on this society when your education is complete."

Sal could see that Jeff was considering his words carefully. "What's on your mind, Jeff?" he asked. "How do you feel about what's happened to you in such a short time? Give me your gut reaction."

"I don't know if I have a gut reaction," Jeff began. "I think it's more of a heartfelt reaction. My heart is overwhelmed. I've tried, from the day I met Mrs. Merrill, to make sense of all she's done for me. But I've failed to make any sense of it. My heart says, 'Take what she's giving you and try to emulate her generosity and commitment in your dealings with others.' But my head says, 'Why? Why has she singled me out for all of the good things she's given and continues to give?' How am I supposed to react? What can I say to her that will best express all of the things that I feel?"

Mrs. Merrill entered the restaurant with a broad smile on her face. She was in what appeared to be a very jovial mood.

Jeff told her how happy he was to see her. He tried, as best he could, to heed the advice Sal had given him and to let her do most of the talking. This was hard because there were so many things Jeff was dying to say on what would be his last visit with her for a long time. He hated the idea of holding back at this critical moment.

"Have you guys been drinking too much while waiting for me?" she asked.

"We're sober and on our best behavior," Sal said as he discretely left the table.

"This is quite a day in our journey," Mrs. Merrill mused, "but each journey has a beginning and an end. Our initial journey is coming to an end. But, for you, a new journey begins. You're pretty well focused now and I urge you to remain that way. You have the ability to achieve anything you wish to achieve. I challenge you to aim high but to keep your feet on the ground. You've been through hard times and there may be more to come. Just understand and remember that for each problem, there is a solution. For each dark cloud, there is a rainbow. And, for each evil human being that would do you harm, there are countless others who wish you well. Tomorrow, you'll leave here and you'll begin a new phase in your life. You've given your best for your country. Now, you must give yourself no less. I won't go to the train station to see you off, but I hope that you know I'll be there in spirit and in prayer."

Jeff started to say something, but she stopped him abruptly. "The power of your silence, at this point, is more meaningful to

me than any words," she said. "Your eyes tell me all I need to
know. Let's just have an enjoyable dinner and think about what
has been and what's to come. One last reminder," she said, "let me
hear from you often."

As Jeff left the restaurant, a thousand thoughts consumed him.
He had said none of the things he wanted to say. Mrs. Merrill had
stopped him before he could even begin to speak. He knew that
she had her reasons for not wanting him to speak but he felt that
he should have insisted on having his say.

On the ferry back to Manhattan, Jeff tried to be calm and to
put this meeting in perspective. But try as he may, nothing eased
the pain he felt for not sharing his gratitude for all that that Mrs.
Merrill had done for him. His whole life had been changed because
she had come along. The train to Nashville would be leaving in
less than twelve hours and he was so anxious that sleeplessness was
a certainty.

He was sure that Aunt Lila would be sleeping when he arrived
home. This pleased him because, as much as he loved Aunt Lila,
he was in no mood for conversation. The final conversation with
Mrs. Merrill had sapped his energy. In some ways, he felt like he
had attended a wake. A chapter in his life had come to an abrupt
end. This woman had taught him, advised him, scolded him and
praised him. She had laughed and cried with him. Now he was
leaving her. It was not an easy thing to do.

Jeff used the time on the long train ride from New York to
Nashville to attempt to put all of the things that had happened
over the past four years in proper perspective. What, four years
earlier, had been a life without hope had now evolved into a life
that held promise. Jeff still had misgivings about his ability to do
college work, but Mrs. Merrill had repeatedly said that he was
focused, disciplined and capable. He had been forced to become a
man at an early age. She insisted that this could work to his
advantage. "Don't be afraid to seek help if you need it," was her
message. "Ask questions, listen for answers, and search thoroughly
to be sure the information you are getting is correct," she stressed.

In essence, Jeff reasoned, this had been the same doctrine the

Army had taught him. Gather all of the facts, analyze them, check again, and, when action is required, act swiftly and decisively. Jeff knew that this was what he must continually focus upon if he was to succeed in college and in life. This doctrine had been successful for him when lives were at stake, why not now? Was it not true that another life was again at stake? His own life, he reasoned.

CHAPTER THIRTY

Tennessee State University was a sprawling institution with thousands of students rushing from office to office trying to get registered for their required courses. The dormitories were bustling with activity. Although things seemed, at times, chaotic, there was actually an organized pattern to the activity.

The university had a Veteran's Affairs advisor, Mrs. Carolyn Knight, who assisted and guided former soldiers who were enrolling in college for the first time. Mrs. Knight was an efficient, compassionate, but "no nonsense" administrator who guided hundreds of veterans through the housing and registration processes. Although the federal government, under the newly enacted G.I. Bill of Rights, would pay for tuition and living expenses, the university was not prepared to accommodate the huge demand for its services that was created by the large influx of veterans. Mrs. Knight's job was more than challenging. Dormitory space was at a premium and the surrounding communities had exhausted all of their resources trying to meet the demand for rooms and apartments. Under pressure from the college, the state of Tennessee finally established a trailer park on the university campus. Two— and three-bedroom trailers were transported to the campus from all over the state in order to house the returning veterans. Jeff was assigned a room in one of the two-bedroom trailers.

On his first day of classes, Jeff began to appreciate the magnitude of the change that this new world of Tennessee State had brought to his life. The United States Army had been good to him and good for him. But the Army was a regimented, segregated world. Yes, nonwhite soldiers who showed ability and leadership could be recognized and rewarded. But the fact remained that the power structure to which Jeff was accustomed was all white. At this sprawling university, the power structure was black. For the first time in his life, Jeff saw a black segment of American society that was different than any he had ever known.

The university president was a tall, elegant black man who had the respect of the entire college community as well as the respect of power brokers across the state of Tennessee. President Walters was a learned man with a Ph.D. from one of America's most elite institutions. In spite of his high status, President Walters was approachable. He was especially sensitive to the needs and aspirations of the returning veterans. He made it known that the university was prepared to do whatever it took to assure their success. In addition to President Walters, there were dozens of black professors with Ph.D.s who were able and willing to extend a hand to any student in need of help.

Professor Merl Epps, the Chairman of the History department, was impressed with Jeff and with the things he had accomplished since leaving rural Alabama just a few years earlier. Professor Epps was a published author and an outspoken critic of the manner in which the black role in America's life and history had been ignored. Professor Epps' first book began to explore the important role black people had played in settling and growing America. As Jeff read this book, he thought he could now begin to understand the part he had played in the deadly drama called World War II. In a society as vast and complex as America, each contribution, no matter how small, adds to the whole. "It is our ability to recognize individual contributions that enables us to see the big picture," he concluded. He began to appreciate the fact that America had been able to evolve from an agricultural society, an agrarian economy, to a world economic and political power, in significant measure because its economy had been built, for years, on the backs of four million slaves who demonstrated individual and collective strength that was beyond measure.

Professor Epps exchanged letters with Mrs. Merrill during the first year Jeff was at the university. Both agreed that, in order to satisfy his curiosity about other black or "colored" people, Jeff needed to know the role that his ancestors had played in sharing

America's past as well as the role they continue to play in shaping its future. It was at this point that Jeff decided to pursue a degree in History and Political Science.

The more deeply involved Jeff became in the history and politics of America, the more he realized that the history books had been written with the view that America was primarily a nation made up of Anglo-Saxon Protestant whites. If other ethnic groups existed, their roles were apparently deemed not worthy of recognition and inclusion.

Professor Epps' research and documentation refuted the perspective of mainstream historians, as reflected in their writings. In his writings, Professor Epps laid out the fact that, while many ethnic groups had helped to build America, only the contributions of those of white, western European ancestry had been acknowledged. The very real contributions of blacks and others had been ignored.

The world of academia was an amazing new experience for Jeff. He became so focused and so immersed in his studies and in the faculty around him that a social life was not a priority. At the end of his junior year, his grade point average was 3.7. In her letters and telephone calls, Mrs. Merrill reminded him that, while she was very proud of his academic achievements, he needed to interact more with the students and the faculty.

"Continue to build your people skills; enhance your communication skills; learn to be a good speaker," she admonished. "All of the knowledge you are acquiring will be of little value unless you can communicate it, unless you can relate to the world around you."

In an effort to improve his communications skills, Jeff joined the university debating team, he accompanied Professor Epps on many of his speaking engagements and he became a stagehand in the university's little theater. Under the guidance of Mrs. Merrill and Professor Epps, it seemed that Jeff was beginning to rid himself of the little doubts that had plagued him when he first arrived at the university. He had taken full course loads each semester and he had attended summer school for the past two years. At the end of the present semester he would achieve senior status. He was on his way to graduation in two more semesters.

A sense of pride surged through him as he pondered the thought of being a college graduate. Late at night, Jeff's mind would drift back in time to the events that helped to catapult him to this place. College had never been a goal in his life. He had been led to believe that his would always be a world of subservience to white folks. He would always be seen as a "boy", at the beck and call of his "masters".

But Mama Essie had always said to him, "You don't know what God has in mind for you. Just be patient and be ready to accept God's challenge when he reveals Himself to you."

Well, it now seemed to him that God had challenged him and he was trying as best as he could to meet that challenge. Was it an accident that had caused him to walk into the Staten Island library? Did Mrs. Merrill just happen to be there? Did she decide on the spur of the moment to intervene in his life? Or was this his destiny, brought about by a force so great that it was beyond his ability to fully understand? Whatever it was, Jeff was very careful to avoid the arrogance of believing he had come this far based solely on his own abilities. He knew that no one could make this perilous journey, from where he had been to where he was now, alone. Mama Essie, Mrs. Merrill, Father Morrelli, Professor Epps, and the force of the United States Army—all seemed to come together and bring him to this point. Jeff finished his education three years after entering the university.

Jeff called Mrs. Merrill in New York. She was very pleased and excited. Her excitement came through loud and clear over the telephone. She asked when he would be returning to New York and said that she and Sal were planning a celebration for him. Jeff promised that he would be in New York within the next five days and that he would call her as soon as he arrived.

The train ride back to New York was very different from the one he had taken to Nashville three years before. A sense of excitement and great joy had, it seemed, taken control of his body, his mind, and, indeed, his spirit.

On this trip, Jeff was seated next to a woman who was returning to her home in Baltimore. She had just attended a three-day meeting at the National Baptist Convention Headquarters in Nashville. During the long train ride, Jeff told his traveling companion about his background. He explained how he had been mentored, counseled, and advised by Mrs. Merrill. The woman tilted back in her seat, closed her eyes and smiled. She urged Jeff to continue, saying, "This is interesting. I need to hear more."

At times, when Jeff was almost certain that the woman had fallen asleep, she would clap her hands lightly and urge him to continue with the story. Two hours into the discussion, Jeff was struck by a thought. "I never seem to be able to tell this story fully. Each time I talk about my experience I find something new to tell."

The woman abruptly brought her seat to the upright position, tapped Jeff on the shoulder and asked, "Do you believe in a Supreme Being?"

"Yes, I do," was Jeff's reply.

"It seems," the woman continued, "that this Supreme Being, whatever you perceive Him to be, has assigned to you, an angel. Do you believe that there are angels here on earth?" the woman asked. His discussion with Mama Essie on this same subject suddenly came back to him.

"I don't know," he replied.

"Believe it," she said, "There are angels here on earth. But we get so caught up in thoughts of our own power and our own importance that we fail to recognize what should be obvious. I believe you have been given an angel. How else can you account for all of the incredibly good things that have happened to you? Think long and hard about your good fortune and maybe you'll be granted the wisdom to see this woman for what she really is. Now let me get some sleep while you ponder this thought," she concluded.

Jeff leaned back in his seat. He tried to make sense of what the woman had said. In reality, her words were not really very different from the thoughts that had gone through his mind many times over the years. Mama Essie had often referred to Mrs. Merrill as "that angel of a woman". Now here was another person with a very strong belief that an angel had been sent to guide him on his way to a meaningful life here on earth. He needed to give this a lot of thought. With all of these unanswered questions weighing on his mind, Jeff fell asleep. When he awoke, the woman who had been sitting next to him was gone. The train was well past Baltimore. He had no recollection of the stop at Baltimore nor did he have knowledge of the woman leaving the train. But she was gone, and he would be in New York very soon.

Aunt Lila was pleased that Jeff had successfully completed college and she was happy that he had come back to New York. They talked until well past midnight and Jeff told her that he was unsure where he would settle down. Nor had he had made a decision regarding the kind of employment he would seek.

Early in the afternoon, Jeff placed a call to Mrs. Merrill. She was still happy that he had his degree in hand and that he was back in New York. She said that she would call Sal and see if they could get together for dinner that same night. "You have to bring me up to date on everything," she said.

Jeff arrived at Sal's restaurant at eight o'clock sharp. Mrs. Merrill and Sal were already seated. After a period of tearful embraces, Sal ordered a double of bourbon and ginger ale for Jeff. As was her custom, Mrs. Merrill entered her objection to the bourbon, but this time the objection was a mild one. After a period of questions, mostly from Mrs. Merrill, dinner was served. There was more talk after dessert. Jeff knew that he had completed the goals she had set for him and he was determined, once again, to try to express his appreciation for all she had done for him. He wanted her to know what her presence in his life meant to him.

Jeff began by saying, "I can never find the right words to thank you."

With an icy stare and flashing eyes, Mrs. Merrill stopped him in mid-sentence. "I've told you before, I don't need you to thank me," she said, "I need you to pay me. You owe me and I want to be paid."

Jeff sat before this woman in stunned silence. His body was rigid and his stomach reacted as if it had been tied into a knot. Tears started to well in his eyes and he tried to avoid looking in her face. She too was crying. "Well," she said, "how are you going to pay me?"

Jeff's spine stiffened and he spoke like a soldier responding to a command that was out of context with military protocol. "Mrs. Merrill," he shouted, "I have been out of college for less than two weeks. I don't have a job yet, and I don't have any money. When I . . ."

"Stop," she demanded, "stop where you are! For a college graduate, young man, you are awfully dumb. This is not now nor has it ever been about money. It's about going out into the world and being the best that you can be at whatever it is you do—not so much better than everyone else, but the best you can be. Give to others what has been given to you. When you have done that, you pay yourself. When you pay yourself, you've paid me in full."

Sal sat at the table staring into space. Without looking at either of them he said in a trembling voice, "I'm going, I don't have to sit here and listen to you guys argue about who owes who what."

Mrs. Merrill patted Sal on the hand and said, "Sal, I know that, in your world, men don't cry and I respect that. However, I want to tell you that it's all right to cry sometimes. It shows your humanity."

Sal dabbed at his eyes with his napkin and left the table. Jeff, too, prepared to leave. Mrs. Merrill turned to him and started to speak in a soft, almost inaudible voice.

"You and I," she said, "have been bound together for the past six or seven years by a force greater than both of us. I hope the bond between us will never be broken, but now I must let you go. You have the resolve, the strength and the skills to do what you'd like. You have wings now. You can fly on your own power. I'll always remember you, but now, I must let you go."

As Mrs. Merrill walked with him to the door, Jeff turned to her and asked, "Are you an angel?"

She smiled and answered, "I am what you perceive me to be."

CHAPTER THIRTY-ONE

Jeff spent the next week with Aunt Lila. She encouraged him to apply for a civil service job with the City of New York. He considered the possibility, but he could not dismiss from his mind something Mrs. Merrill had admonished him to do. "Give to others what has been given to you." He did not believe that he would be able to do this in a mundane City job.

Mama Essie had told him about a school for veterans and their families that had just opened in his hometown. She urged him to come home and explore the possibility of teaching there. The idea of helping other veterans further their education appealed to Jeff. He believed that he understood, as well as anyone, the crushing weight of ignorance and the embarrassing stigma of not being able to read and write.

"Maybe," Jeff reasoned, "this would be a way to begin to give back what's been given to me."

The director of the veteran's school welcomed Jeff, gave him a tour and urged him to accept a teaching position there. Jeff did accept the position and he soon began teaching reading and math skills to both older and younger veterans. Some of his students had minimal, very minimal, reading and writing abilities; others were totally illiterate.

The job was challenging and required great patience, but for Jeff, it was extremely rewarding. Watching the eyes of forty-five—and fifty-year-old men light up as they read and understood a paragraph in a book for the first time in their lives was very comforting. Some veterans would come to his home on Saturday and Sunday to further enhance their skills. Jeff saw himself in many of those whom he taught. They were eager to learn, but they had never been given an opportunity to learn. As Jeff had done when he first met Mrs. Merrill, many of his students poured out their hearts in expressing their desire to know more about their past. What had life been like for their great-grandparents and their great-great-grandparents? As one seasoned veteran, who called himself "Bo", said, "There must be something written somewhere about us, but how will I ever know until I learn to read?"

Eddie, another veteran, had managed to buy a small house with the little money he saved during his four years of Army service. But he was frustrated. He wanted desperately to be able to vote, but his right to vote was repeatedly denied. "I'm a property owner," he complained, "and that qualifies me to vote. The woman at the courthouse shoved some papers in front of me and said, 'Read this and tell me what it means.' I told her that I couldn't read.

"'If you can't read and tell me what you've read, you can't vote,' she said. Then she turned her back and walked away from me. Can you help me to learn how to read?" Eddie pleaded.

Bo and Eddie were two among many veterans who came to the school seeking to learn to read. They believed that education was the key that would unlock the door to a better life for themselves and their families. For two years, Jeff was immersed in the task of doing what he could to combat the ignorance in the lives of the men and women he taught. It was not an easy job. He kept reminding himself that Mrs. Merrill had not, perhaps, had an easy job with him. But she kept going until she was satisfied that her efforts had made a difference in his life. Jeff surmised that living up to her example and dedicating himself to the progress of his students was what Mrs. Merrill meant when she said, "You owe me, and I want to be paid." He realized that this was a debt that he may never be able to fully repay. But he was compelled to try.

At the end of two years, Bo and Eddie, along with dozens of others, were reading, solving simple arithmetic problems, and doing so much more. The biggest change Jeff noticed in the group was how they felt about themselves. There was an air of quiet confidence about each of them. Eddie had gone back to the courthouse. He read that part of the Bill of Rights given to him and he became a registered voter with all rights and the privileges that came with his new status. Bo was struggling, but he was determined to read the history of the United States from 1750 to 1865.

Jeff thought that he saw a very different look in the eyes of many others. The most noticeable difference among all of these students was their attitude. They were beginning to acquire a feeling of self-worth and to develop positive attitudes about their ability to learn and to develop. There were setbacks, to be sure, but the steps forward far outnumbered the setbacks. Jeff was able to bring teachers from other districts into the school to help reinforce what had been taught in the classroom. In addition, clergymen, a lawyer, prominent black businessmen and businesswomen were among some of the people who spoke to and encouraged the class.

In 1950, approximately three years after President Truman had issued an Executive Order desegregating the Armed Forces of the United States, Communist Korean forces moved across the 38th Parallel into South Korea. This action set in motion what President Truman called a "police action" in response to the Chinese aggression. American troops were prepared and they were designated to see military action in defense of South Korea.

It had been more than four years since Jeff had been separated from active duty in the United States Army. Although he was a reserve officer on inactive status, he had no real concern that he would be called to active duty. After all, the president had said that this was a "police action". Nothing in the president's statement made mention of war.

As the weeks and months passed, it became increasingly clear that it made little difference what labels were used—American military personnel were being deployed to South Korea and soon some would be dying. The brewing situation concerned Jeff, just as it concerned most veterans who had come home from Europe and Asia. Hundreds of thousands had either built or were beginning to build new homes. Many thousands more were enrolled in schools and colleges or they had embarked upon new careers. Many were raising families. Now the trumpets of war were sounding again and, as any soldier, sailor, airman or marine knows, when the trumpet sounds, you respond.

Jeff's status changed from "inactive" to "active reserve" and he was recalled to active duty. His orders directed him to report to the commanding officer at Fort Dix, New Jersey. His arrival on this post as an officer was far different than his arrival at Fort Benning, Georgia, almost a decade before. He now felt confident and self-assured as he stood before his new commander. After his orientation and assignment to quarters, Jeff visited the officers' club. Present at the club were a half dozen or more black officers, including a major and two lieutenant colonels. "What a difference a decade makes," he thought, "especially in the military services of the United States."

Jeff was sent to a series of military schools for a period of sixteen weeks. Upon completion of his training, he was assigned to an infantry training regiment at Fort Dix. The unit's mission was to prepare young soldiers for combat in Korea.

Watching the newly inducted eighteen-and nineteen-year-old soldiers in training reminded Jeff of his own experiences years before. But as he watched, he got the feeling that the men drafted for service in Korea were a little different from those who had served during World War II. These men were, without a doubt, generally better educated and more informed about the world around them than he and his fellow soldiers had been. Despite this educational advantage, most of the new draftees had never heard of the Korean peninsula. Those who had heard of it often did not see the situation there as a threat to the national security of the United States. It was difficult to explain to these soldiers why it was in the country's national interest to be so deeply involved in this "police action" in a far-off place. Jeff had questions of his own on that front.

The President of the United States called the Korean conflict a "police action" and perhaps it was. But the news out of Korea told the nation that young Americans were bleeding and dying on the battlefields of the Korean peninsula in numbers that were staggering, even from the perspective of battle-seasoned soldiers. World War II still seemed fresh in the minds of many. Early in the nineteen fifties, before the muted sounds of the war of the previous decade had drifted into the distance, the call to arms had sounded again—a call to arms that was anticipated by almost no one.

While there was no hesitation on his part to answer the call for further military service, Jeff's mindset was far different than it had been at the time he had enlisted in World War II. He was no longer a teenager. He had grown tremendously from his experiences. He now saw the world around him in a very different light. Public support for this "police action" was not the same as the support the nation had given its troops during World War II.

As he thought about it, Jeff began to understand one of the reasons that he approached this new challenge from a very different perspective. When he had first enlisted in the United States Army, he knew little about the history or political dynamics of the countries that had been engaged in war. He was very young and painfully uneducated. However, he did understand that his service in Europe had been in support of an important cause. He knew that that cause and the principles upon which it was based had world support. Korea, it seemed to him, was simply a civil war, a war being waged by two very different factions of the same country. He wasn't really sure what purpose his participation was serving.

The President of the United States had concluded that the national security was at risk. Although Jeff did not agree, it was certainly beyond the ability or the right of a foot soldier to question the Commander in Chief. Like all of those who had been called upon to serve, Jeff did so without hesitation. But his enthusiasm for being a soldier was not the same as it had been during World War II. Jeff believed that he was as patriotic as any. But while he prepared for this assignment, he found himself increasingly resenting the fact that he had, again, been called upon to help bring peace and freedom to a country that was not his own. He was expected to help free another country's people from tyranny while the tyranny that his own people, in his own country, faced was being ignored. The freedoms that he was called upon to help defend in Korea were freedoms that he did not know, freedoms he had never enjoyed in the country of his birth. His people still did not have the right to vote, the right to a good education, the right to good health care or, in reality, the right to be and feel secure in the places they called "home".

Although he had served his country in the greatest of all wars, he, along with millions of other black Americans, was forced to sit in the back of buses and trains, to drink from separate water fountains. In much of the country, he could not eat in a restaurant of his choice. All of these indignities were sanctioned and enforced by state laws. The sovereign state of Alabama, in the nineteen fifties, had its own "police action". That "police action" focused on arresting anyone who sought to challenge the "white only" scheme of things. Jeff knew that he was seen as a lesser person in his native state, but he also knew that he was seen as an equal in the United States Army. He tried to put all of these thoughts behind him for a while. He focused his thoughts on three things—what Mama Essie believed he could become, what the United States Army had allowed, even encouraged, him to become and what Mrs. Merrill had insisted that he become. These three factors were cogent reasons for him to answer this recent call to arms just four and a half short years after the end of World War II. But he had to wonder, "Did America have its priorities in order?"

The troubling thoughts that Jeff had about his service in Korea were thoughts he kept to himself. It was true that the Army that he was reporting to now was a far different Army than the one he had left after World War II. Gone were the segregated units, led almost exclusively by white officers. He was now reporting to a fully integrated United States Army, one in which competence mattered more than color. In many ways, the military had come of age. It had given dignity, respect and opportunity to many who had not been privy to such in the past. However, despite this dramatic change, there were still few black officers in the military and even fewer black officers in Korea. Certainly, Jeff could not speak about his thoughts to his white commanders and the black officers who served in Korea were spread out over a wide area. There was little or no opportunity for contact among them.

Was there, Jeff wondered, at least a lesson he could learn from his service in Korea? Or would he have been more productive if he had remained at home and used this time to help fashion a nonviolent plan to impact his own people, in his own country? Would this extended stay out of the country and away from home dampen his desire to help secure the changes that he knew were important?

Mrs. Merrill had taught Jeff to be prepared for any and all things that he sought to do. She had said on countless occasions, "Be certain that your goals are right and just, and pursue them relentlessly. Use your brain and moral persuasion to achieve your goals," she had preached.

On his deathbed, Father Morrelli had insisted that Jeff read and memorize a passage from the Bible, "Unto everything there is a season."

"The season for your greatest achievement is yet to be," he said. "Great victories are won by great ideas. When you're certain that you have formulated the best ideas possible, move forward. Let nothing deter you. If defeat comes on the first try, try again and again. You will be successful," he had said. "Guns and bombs can defeat armies but they cannot stifle great ideas. Righteousness must be your cause. You must wish for others all of the good things that you wish for yourself. Never compromise your good intentions for political expediency."

Were Father Morrelli's words still true? Over recent years, Father Morrelli had been in Jeff's thoughts more often than usual. Jeff remembered that, minutes before his death, Father Morrelli had spoken to him in a voice that seemed far away. Although the priest's voice was weak, the glint in his eyes was brighter than usual.

"I predict good things for you," he said. "No," he corrected himself, "I predict great things for you. If you believe in the truths that I have endeavored to reveal to you, then you will go about your life and fulfill my prophecy."

As Jeff had started to leave the priest's bedside that last day, Mrs. Merrill had taken his arm and led him back. Father Morrelli motioned Jeff to come closer. Jeff leaned over the bedside in order to hear the faint words that were coming from deep inside a man whose earthly life was slipping away. The priest was struggling to make his words audible.

"My son," he said, "don't allow any person to cause you to become cynical, to hate or to do destructive things. Dedicate yourself to building bridges among people. Build bridges that lead to better relationships among the races. Don't worry if you're misunderstood by some. A personality greater than you or I was vastly misunderstood. But that did not stop His good work. Now go out into the world around you. Do good work. Someday your inheritance will be great. Go now," he said, "and follow your rainbow."

After three years of service in Korea, Jeff was coming home. He was proud of his service, both in Korea and in Europe, but he was deeply disturbed about conditions at home. The availability of decent jobs for black Americans was almost nonexistent. In the South, segregation was still rigidly enforced. Despite having served his country for more than eight years in two separate wars, Jeff and millions like him still could not register to vote. Decent housing was difficult to obtain. Despite being a decorated military officer, Jeff would still have to sit in the back of the bus. Some whites would still call him "boy", even though they knew of his honorable service in two wars.

He was also deeply disturbed about the big battles yet to be waged—the battle for recognition as a decent human being; the battle to enjoy the same rights and privileges that were guaranteed to white Americans. Jeff was not looking for any special favors. He wanted only what was guaranteed to others by the Constitution of the United States. As matters now stood, the United States government that he had faithfully served was saying to him and millions of others, "You, as black people, are not equal to the rest of us."

Jeff rejected this whole doctrine of segregation. He believed that if, indeed, he had been equal enough to fight for the rights of people in far-off places, equal enough to defend the rights of a country he had rarely heard of prior to nineteen fifty, then he was equal enough to have access to all of the rights and responsibilities associated with full citizenship in the country of his birth. In his mind, there was no doubt that he was about to engage himself in the most important battle of his life.

He had seen enough physical violence to know that it was not the answer to America's problems at home. This fight had to be different; it had to be a fight of ideas—ideas based on moral righteousness and human decency. This fight, in Jeff's view, could not rely upon lethal weapons, secret codes or stealth operations. This fight had to be waged in the open, with its mission clearly stated. It could not be waged for the purpose of gaining an unfair advantage over any segment of the population; and it could not, it must not, be waged to suppress anyone. Indeed, in the final analysis, this battle must free everyone or it would be a battle lost.

In this looming unrest, there would be no generals directing the action from a central command post. This battle would be waged in the minds and the hearts of the American populace. The schools, the mosques, the churches and the synagogues would all be notable participants. According to Jeff's reasoning, this fight would be a long one. He knew many Americans, both black and white, who feared that the battle for equal rights in America would never end. Although he, too, was uncertain of the outcome, Jeff knew that this was a battle that must begin and he knew that, somehow, he had to play a role.

As he tried to figure out how he could contribute to the struggle, Jeff recalled his last hours in Korea. While sitting in the terminal at Kimpo Airport, just outside of the capital city of Seoul, South Korea, Jeff had been acutely aware of the conversations taking place all around him. The flight home had been delayed several hours. Officers were discussing what was in store for them when they arrived home. Some officers talked about the job opportunities in business and industry that would be open to them; others talked about going into politics or working for federal, state or local government. A few of the officers talked about establishing consulting firms that would help shape policies that would be vital to protecting America's interests in the ensuing years.

Listening to the various conversations going on around him,

Jeff became somewhat depressed. The opportunities that these white officers spoke about would not be available to him. The thought of going back to his native Alabama only made his depression worse. While others spoke about their futures with hope, Jeff knew that, for him, yet another challenge was forming. He was certain that returning to Alabama, as he had done after World War II, was not the answer. This time, he decided to settle in Newark, New Jersey.

CHAPTER THIRTY-TWO

Although New Jersey was not as rigidly segregated as Alabama was, equal opportunity still proved to be an elusive concept for most of its black citizens. In Newark, the state's largest city, the housing stock, as well as the public school system were deteriorating rapidly. The city was beginning to experience "white flight"— middle-class and affluent whites leaving the city for more exclusive and more homogeneous communities in the suburbs. With this phenomenon, Newark's healthy tax base was rapidly disappearing. Funding for the local school district had been reduced. Manufacturing and office jobs that had once been a lifeline for local residents began to move to places that were not so easily reached by Newark's vast labor pool.

In the nineteen fifties, Newark's city government was not particularly sensitive to the needs of its black citizenry. Despite the city's huge black population, there was no black representation in city government. That would not come until late in the decade. Newark, New Jersey was, by no stretch of the imagination, as hostile and formally segregated as the state of Alabama. There were no laws mandating separate but so-called equal facilities. But covert segregation was the order of the day. There were clearly "black" communities and "white" communities within the city. Anyone who had spent more than a few days in the area knew where these neighborhoods were.

Over the years, black resentment began to build. The feeling of being ignored grew, as did the feeling of being brutalized by the local police. Finally, in 1967, Newark exploded in violence. It was one of many centers of racial violence around the country. These explosions brought a nation's hidden turmoil to the surface and to the headlines. The issues that had been talked about for years in black communities nationwide were now laid bare before a nation at war with itself. This was not a war for territorial expansion as had been faced in Europe, the Far East, and, most recently, in Korea. This was a war for equal rights as spelled out in the Constitution of the United States of America.

Many people asked why it was that minorities who had fought and died on battlefields worldwide were not entitled to the same kind of liberation that they had helped to achieve in far away places. This was one of the personal dilemmas Jeff faced as he tried to settle into a new life.

In all of this turmoil, Jeff still knew that his most effective role would not be found in the violent streets. His military experience had taught him that violence could often not be avoided; in fact, there were times when it was necessary. But he had experienced enough violence. He could not go down that path again. He had to impact this battle in a different way.

Mrs. Merrill had preached constantly about education and the need to be informed. She was resolute in her belief that education was the solution to the many ills that plagued the nation. She was determined that Jeff would use his education not just to enrich himself, but also to teach, to inform others.

"You have an obligation, a duty, to try to do for others what many people have done for you. Go out there," she said, "and help eliminate the ignorance that cripples many young people. Yours," she continued, "has been a life that has seen its share of poverty, discrimination, and exclusion. Sheer determination on your part has lifted you to a new level. It would be shameful if you did not go out and give to others what has been given to you."

"To everything there is a season," Father Morrelli had said. A season of upheaval and violence had left Jeff shaken and perplexed. What could he do to make a difference, to help usher in a new season?

In Montgomery, Alabama, a young minister had suddenly come on the national scene. His message was grounded in nonviolent activism. He believed that one could resist oppression and achieve civil rights even while being nonviolent. Martin Luther King, Jr.

openly opposed the practice of segregation on buses and in public facilities. He and his followers had won a resounding victory on this issue before the Supreme Court of the United States. Although violence had repeatedly been visited upon him and his followers, they had remained nonviolent in their response. Like many other Americans, Jeff had been deeply touched by the strategy and the courageous actions of this young minister. Like many veterans who had fought, been injured or watched others die in war, Jeff started to realize the ancient truth of the words, "He who lives by the sword, will, in the end, die by the sword."

Violence produced more violence. The cycle had to be stopped, he reasoned. Father Morrelli had said that if you come forth with good ideas, and if you use these good ideas to lift and advance the cause of humanity, all of the armies of the world will be powerless against you. Martin Luther King, Jr. seemed to be a living example of the father's words.

"Armed men," Father Morrelli had said, "can kill the body, but not the spirit."

All of the ideas Mrs. Merrill and Father Morrelli had instilled in him over the years now began to have much deeper meaning. Sometimes he felt as if they were whispering instructions to him, although he knew they were not there.

Jeff truly believed that his skills were in teaching. He felt that he had done a good job of teaching veterans to read and to write while employed at a special school in his hometown in Alabama. He believed he could use those skills again.

"Knowledge is power," he reasoned, "and unless and until we get the knowledge, power will be just an illusion."

Jeff realized that education was an ongoing process. The more you learned, the more you needed to learn. Education, he thought, could be compared to a rainbow—it seemed so near, but one never got close enough to capture it in its totality. He knew that he must continue to pursue educational opportunities in the same manner that military commanders pursued the enemy on the battlefield. If ignorance was the enemy, it made sense that it must be attacked relentlessly. In the military, Jeff had watched some of the best commanders plan their strategy. Identify the enemy, locate the enemy, and decide what resources are needed to defeat the enemy. Assemble the resources, formulate a plan, and finally, execute the plan to its final conclusion. Ignorance, Jeff concluded, was the enemy that had faced him and millions like him. Even though he had taught in Alabama and believed that he had achieved a modicum of success there, Jeff knew that, in order to achieve greater success, he needed to acquire more knowledge, more skills.

Consulting with Mrs. Merrill, his greatest advisor, he shared his thoughts. As they sat in her office talking, a broad smile crossed Mrs. Merrill's face.

"Jeff, you have come into your own. If I hear you correctly, your passion is teaching. I believe you should identify the college or university best suited to give you the additional training you need to become a successful teacher. When you've done this, enroll there and don't just be satisfied to get a decent grade. We both know that you'll have little or no difficulty getting good grades. Beyond the grades, you need to find something that will help you to create in your students a thirst for knowledge. I have no specific name for that 'something'. I suppose it's a combination of many things—good teaching skills, a passion for imparting knowledge, and a belief that every student has the capacity to learn. I believe that these are the intangibles that make a good teacher a great teacher. If this is what you aspire to, then I say, get down to the business of fulfilling your dream."

Trenton State College had a reputation as the best institution in New Jersey for training prospective teachers. Jeff enrolled there. During his first semester at Trenton State, he realized that he had made the right choice. The curriculum to which he was exposed and the teaching strategies and techniques that he learned vastly expanded his horizon. But he also realized there were critical teaching qualities that could only be learned through experience. These were qualities that even the best college professors just could not teach. This was the "something" that Mrs. Merrill had referred to. Jeff thought that this "something" was comprised of ideas, habits and attitude. Using these guideposts, he tried to formulate new ideas to stimulate learning. He endeavored to instill good work habits in those he taught. Attitude, he believed, was the key to unlocking closed minds. He tried always to adopt the attitude that, under the right circumstances, every child and every adult can learn. And every person can impart what he or she learns to others. The right attitude, he believed, was found in the saying, "Each one can teach one."

From the mid-nineteen fifties, when Jeff arrived in Newark, through the early nineteen sixties, it was not easy for a black person, especially a black male, to secure a teaching position in any New Jersey school system. Boards of education and their human resource departments were predominantly white. Urban school populations, however, were becoming increasingly black. New Jersey school systems, unlike those in Alabama, were not segregated by statute. But it was painfully obvious to those who cared to look that covert segregation was the rule. Its effect was just as damaging as and was far more insidious than segregation that had been ordered by law. Much of white America still clung to the antebellum theory of manifest destiny. This theory embraced the idea that black America was the white man's burden. It advanced the belief that black people were incapable of self-determination, that they would forever be a burden that white America was forced to carry. Carrying that burden was and would forever remain white America's "Christian duty".

Mama Essie had summed it up most correctly when she said, "A heap of attitudes will have to change before we get over this hurdle." A heap of attitudes had not changed by the beginning of the decade of the nineteen sixties.

Mrs. Merrill had previously commented that attitudes don't just change. Someone or something had to cause them to change; even then, the process was slow. Jeff felt an overwhelming obligation to begin the process of trying to change enough attitudes to make a difference, even a small difference, in the ways people saw and related to each other.

The attitudes of most black Americans were quite different from those of most white Americans. A mythical line had, over the years, been drawn separating the two groups. Was this line based upon logic? Or were these differences the end product of ignorance and learned hatred? No one, Jeff reasoned, is born with hatred. Hatred is learned. But for some to learn something, others must teach it. Ignorance and hatred were the enemies. If one could strike a blow at ignorance, perhaps the races could see each other in a different light.

His military service had taught him to "begin with what you know". One thing Jeff knew very well was how crippling ignorance could be. It robbed individuals of their dignity. It led to inhumane treatment. It caused nations to become bogged down in their own folly. Ultimately it led to death and destruction. At this point, it was clear to Jeff where to focus his efforts. He would become a teacher. If he could not secure a teaching position in the public sector, he would teach on the street, in homes or in churches. Wherever there was an opportunity, he would teach.

His passion for teaching was great, but Jeff still had to pay the rent, put food on the table, and do the other things that were needed to sustain life. While trying to secure a teaching position, he applied for jobs in factories, usually as a janitor or a handyman. In most instances, when he truthfully answered questions about his education, his job application was turned down. Most employers were not interested in hiring a college-educated janitor or factory worker.

Jeff's older brother, Sonny Man, had worked in a large parking garage in downtown Newark for many years. Sensing his younger brother's discouragement, Sonny Man spoke to the garage owner about Jeff. Within a short time, the brothers were working side by side.

Life had taken so many twists and turns. Jeff had gone from a childhood of hopelessness to an unanticipated world of opportunity in the Army; from a time of patriotic commitment to his military duty to a time of unsettling disillusion with a country that would not seem to allow him to call it "his own".

As a child in Alabama, even the thought of a regular job at a parking garage, a decent place to live and regular meals would have seemed so wonderful as to be almost unattainable. But through the eyes of an unexpectedly young, black officer in the United States Army, he would never have anticipated the frustration of the job search that had consumed him for the past several months. He knew that life could not be expected to be an unending series of successes, but he had never anticipated that he would have so much trouble following a dream. At least at this time in his life, he thought, he was able to dream. That luxury had not always been possible.

During the time he worked in the parking garage, Jeff came into contact with many different people. Some people came, went and were never seen again. Some were regular customers. His brother usually took care of the "regulars". One day, Jeff's brother was heavily engaged in a discussion with one of the regular customers about the merits of this year's baseball season. Sonny Man's amiable exchange was with a famous New York Yankees' shortstop who was also a spokesman for one of Newark's large men's clothing stores. Not wanting to interrupt his discussion, Jeff's brother asked him to get the shortstop's car and to put the convertible top down.

"This is my brother," said Sonny Man with pride. "He's an Army guy—was in World War II and Korea. He even went to college, but he's having trouble finding a job. Right now, he's working with me."

"What kind of a job are you looking for?" the famous athlete asked.

"I want to teach, sir," said Jeff. "But I haven't had much luck in that area yet."

"I can't be much help to you there. I don't have many connections in the teaching field, but I do know a few people at National State Bank. If you'd like, I'll speak to someone there. Maybe they have a position for you. Would you like me to do that?"

"Yes, sir, I'd like that," Jeff responded.

A few weeks later, Jeff had the name of a contact at the bank. Shortly thereafter, he had an interview and a job offer to work as a proof operator in the cancelled check department. He wasn't yet in the classroom, but he thought he was getting a little closer.

His hours were from midnight to 8:00 A.M. Over the next year, Jeff worked nights and looked for teaching positions by day. Was this the reality that would continue to plague him and other black veterans who had served their country with honor? Was it indeed "their country" or were they just nomads in a land that would never be their own?

Jeff started to recall the looks on the faces of the people of Saint-Lo, France when the United States Army arrived after crushing German troops at the end of a hard fought battle. An old woman approached Jeff and handed him a bottle of calvados. She kissed him on both cheeks and, with tears running down her face, exclaimed, "Freedom! Freedom! We never knew what freedom meant until the Germans came and we lost our freedom."

During the long days on the streets looking for an opportunity to become a teacher, the image of the old woman in Saint-Lo suddenly appeared before Jeff's eyes. Perhaps the woman had, in the final analysis, fared a lot better than he had. She had once enjoyed freedom, lost it and finally gained it back. Jeff began to realize that he had never really had what this woman once lost. The irony struck without mercy. He and many thousands of other nonwhite soldiers had served their country honorably; many had died to bring to others a freedom that it seemed they would never have at home.

"Don't become cynical and discouraged," he remembered Father Morrelli telling him long ago. "Above all," the priest had said, "don't allow your emotions to blind your vision."

The job at the bank was not the kind of work that Jeff really wanted. He believed that his skills were grossly under utilized, but it certainly was a step up from parking cars all day. The baseball player had been very generous in his dealings with Jeff. He tipped more liberally than any other customer Jeff came in contact with and he was sensitive to Jeff's concerns. The ball player almost always took time to inquire about Jeff's welfare and he encouraged Jeff to hang in there because, as he said, "Things will get better.

"We all have our challenges," he continued. "Some of our challenges are self-imposed, but your challenge is different. You're intelligent, resourceful and energetic. But our society still can't get past the color of your skin."

Jeff continued working at the bank, but the work was dull, repetitive and boring. The pay was notoriously low and there was little, if any chance for advancement. As boring as the job was, it enabled Jeff to pay the rent, put food on the table and, to some degree, keep his hope for something better alive.

While scanning the "Help Wanted" ads in the daily newspapers, Jeff was attracted to an ad for a shipping supervisor at a local manufacturing plant. "The candidate," the ad read, "must be intelligent, self-motivated and must be able to supervise a workforce of fifteen to twenty men." Pay was contingent upon experience and ability. At the interview, Jeff met David, a young chemical engineer who was about Jeff's own age. David was the head of this sprawling family-owned business. He was impressed with Jeff's background and his outlook.

"I believe you can solve the problems we have in our shipping department," David said, "and, if you believe you would like to join us, I'm prepared to make you an attractive offer."

The offer was very attractive. Jeff immediately accepted. The pay was triple the amount he was making at the bank, but the work was demanding and it was dirty. Within the next several weeks, Jeff worked long, hard hours to reorganize shipping procedures. He retrained the personnel within the shipping department and he tried to instill pride in and appreciation for the people who worked in the department. While the shipping supervisor's job was financially rewarding, there was something missing. Jeff still was not doing the kind of work he wanted to do.

After two years, a real break finally came. Jeff applied for and was offered a position as director of tutoring at a nonprofit children's service organization. The pay was extremely low, but the rewards of working with elementary and middle school students to help them acquire reading and math skills more than made up for the low pay.

Watching some of these young people struggle to learn new skills often took Jeff back to his days of being taught at the Staten

Island library by Mrs. Merrill. When he saw the wonder in the eyes of a boy or girl who had acquired and mastered a new skill or a new concept, Jeff knew that his decision to accept this wonderful low-paying job was the right decision. He had come to the place where he wanted to be. He had come home.

CHAPTER THIRTY-THREE

Many things had changed from the days of Jeff's early success and rapid advancement in the military. In many ways, civilian life had proven to be much harder than he had expected. Obstacles that he didn't find in the military presented themselves, but life was never again as hard as the early days in Alabama. Throughout the years, the lasting lessons of his life remained—lessons taught by his mother, his grandmother, Mrs. Merrill and Father Morrelli. None of us makes it through this life alone. Others open doors for us, if we care to see through them, to the possibilities in life. A few of those who open doors are truly angels, but others are just good people, doing good things. The distinction isn't important. We need to learn to recognize and appreciate both. And, as Mrs. Merrill taught, we have an obligation to open a few doors along our own life's journey. We may not all have the capacity to be angels. But we all have the capacity to be good people.

Over the years, Jeff found many opportunities to teach—in public schools and private schools, in large cities and smaller towns. The settings varied greatly, but the challenges were remarkably similar from one community to the next. More than thirty years passed in what, in many ways, seemed like no time at all.

As Jeff retired from teaching and looked forward to a quieter life in a small Connecticut town, the lessons of good people opening doors came home to him again. A casual remark by one of his neighbors about the local elementary school needing volunteers started him on a new and unexpected path, one that rekindled his passion for mentoring. He began to spend one day each week in the classroom of Mrs. Julie Alexander, working with second-grade students who needed extra help. One day became two, two became three. Before long, the district established a formal mentoring program and Jeff began working with older students as well. For several years, he spent some time almost every day in the local schools, working with students who needed that little extra support to reach their potential.

The passion for reaching others through teaching, which Mrs. Merrill had kindled so long ago, had not diminished. Just as he hoped to open doors for others through his commitment to mentoring, others were still opening doors for Jeff as well. After three years of volunteering, Jeff received an unexpected letter from the president of a nearby college. The letter informed him that the college would recognize his life's work by awarding him an honorary Doctor of Humane Letters at the institution's upcoming graduation.

Jeff was stunned. He had started his life in poverty, barely able to go to school at all. Throughout the years—with all of their many challenges and difficult days—circumstances, good people, and faith had made a way for him to move forward. But this was more than he could have ever imagined. Yes, he had tried to make a contribution to this world. But he could not have made that contribution on his talents alone. Others had helped to make it possible. Somehow, he had to make that clear.

On a beautiful sunny afternoon in June, the college faculty made the long, solemn march from the administration building to the quad. The sound of "Pomp and Circumstance" drifted over the entire campus. Standing along the line of march were several of Jeff's most ardent supporters; among them were his granddaughter, Felicia and his grandson, Kevin. Watching, too, as the procession moved slowly toward the quad, was a woman who not only made this day memorable, she, as much as anyone, had made this day possible. Jeff's wife, Janice, stood majestically on the sidelines, watching his every move. The glint in her eyes said, again, what she had said a thousand times before, "Well done!"

As Jeff looked out across an audience of very proud and excited graduating students, surrounded by families and friends, he delivered a message that came from his heart.

"*President Rausch, President Emeritus LaConche,*
members of this great faculty and staff, graduating students, ladies
and gentlemen:
I have about two minutes to say many things that are swirling
through my mind on this very special day. Let me begin by saying
how proud I am to be honored by this great institution.
By your trust and confidence, you have, without a shadow of a
doubt, bestowed upon me the highest honor I could ever receive.
For that, I thank you.

From the cotton fields of Alabama—
to the violent beaches of Normandy—
to the killing grounds of Bastogne—
to the frozen peninsula of Korea—
and, finally, to the hallowed halls of academia—
it has been a long and sometimes perilous journey.
But the truth of the matter is, I did not make this
journey alone.

Permit me, if you will, to pay tribute to my mentor,
to my family, and to friends who have been
instrumental in helping me to get to this place at this time.

Mrs. Anna Marie Merrill—the kind and courageous
New York librarian who gave me the education that
I was denied as a poor child growing up in Alabama—
you are not with us today. But I can see you through
the window of my mind. And I can hear your voice resonating
from the chancellery of heaven and that voice is saying,
'Look at you now!' To Mrs. Merrill, I must say,
'The journey began with you.'

Felicia Wiggins—my granddaughter—you believed that I was a
fairly good storyteller, that I had a message and you urged me
to deliver it. You have helped me to make this journey.

Julie Alexander—for the past three years, you have
been one of my most ardent supporters—and you
have been my friend. You have helped me to make this journey.

And finally—Janice—my wife of 30 years—you have valued my
story and pleaded, urged, cajoled and demanded that I 'go tell it on
the mountain, over the hills and everywhere'.
It is because of you that I am here today.

As we stand here today—on the precipice of the new
millennium—we sometimes realize that the old is a part
of the new. But we also realize that we cannot be satisfied
solely by past achievements. Some may look back and see the past
as 'the good old days'. But the days of old have gone
glimmering—watered by tears, perhaps—but smiled upon by
destiny. Let us move into the 21st century with a new resolve—
with a commitment to ensure that others do not have to
make their journeys through this life alone; with a commitment
that we will give back to life as much or more than we receive;
and with a commitment to adopting new ideas, new habits,
and new attitudes that will help us all to achieve a more just
and humane society. Once again, thank you for this great honor,
and may God bless us all."

His final thoughts, as he received his honorary degree, were of
the words Mama Essie had spoken so many, many years ago. "It's
hard to be a man in a world where the odds are against you. But
you have to find a way to overcome the odds and move forward."
With the help of good people and angels, he had done just that.

Malcolm Zaire Wiggins

EPILOGUE

Malcolm Z. Wiggins arrived on planet Earth at 8:44 P.M. on December 18, 2000, just days before the onset of the new millennium. Malcolm is my great grandson. The society in which he will grow up is a far different society than the one his great grandfather has known.

I hope that Malcolm and all of those with whom he will interact will remember that the old is a part of the new. I trust that he will be a person of great integrity and that he will be compassionate. Most of all, I trust that he will give more than he receives and that he will adopt the ideas of love, peace and justice as guiding stars in a life that offers great rewards.

Overall, America is the greatest place on earth. But if, by chance, Malcolm should ask what advice I leave for him it would be this: "You did not enter a perfect world, but you can help to make it more perfect. Your life will be what you wish it to be if you have a vision and the tenacity to make it so. And, finally, look for unfulfilled promises and make them a reality. In the words of someone wiser than your great grandfather, recognize what life is all about and 'bring to it the rainbow'."

With great expectation, your great grandfather,

Jeff

Jefferson Wiggins can be reached through the Wiggins Institute for Social Integrity in Ridgefield, CT.

He can also be reached via e-mail at jeff@wisi.org.